A tribute to a warrior

"The Dirty Old Indian" MY CANADIAN HERO

By

Tom Sindlinger

"May the sun and the truth shine everywhere"

(Mike Mountain Horse[1])

Published by

2514537 Alberta Society

(Creating, developing, and producing
Alberta literary and theatrical originals)

Second Edition 2025

Ebook ISBN 978-1-966948-13-1

Paperback ISBN 978-1-963100-99-0

Hardcover ISBN 978-1-966948-14-8

---

[1] BURKITT, THYRZA, *Indian Soldier Recalls Pioneer Days*, Calgary Herald, December 26, 1936

"This story is a product of its times.
It talks about prejudices
that were wrong then and remain unacceptable today.

"Rather than ignoring past discriminatory practices,
talking about this story
allows us to engage in thought and discussion
that educates and promotes
the importance of social justice and inclusivity."
(PBS TV, Spokane)

(see what the title means, Page 19)

It is about a highly commendable and courageous Canadian
who was wounded three times in the First World War
and at one time buried for four days by a shell explosion.

He was elected a Chief of his tribe and
a president of a railway labour union local
— an astonishing achievement for his era —

The story is set during a time when Indigenous People
were referred to as Indians
and therefore that name is used for historical truth.

Additionally, Canada's Indians were governed,
as they still are, by the *"Indian Act"*.

The Act is the source of flagrant institutionalized discrimination
that legally perpetuates the word Indian.

**"MIKE MOUNTAIN HORSE was a man ahead of his time
….. a scholar and historian …..
when most Indians were still learning the rudiments."**

Hugh A. Dempsey

Order of Canada, Chief Curator Emeritus of Glenbow Museum
Author of 20 books focused on Blackfoot history

Foreword

The history of *Mike Mountain Horse* is a powerful and worthy story that deserves to be told, retold and shared.

Mike Mountain Horse's life of a leader, a soldier, a labourer, a union-worker, a family man and so much more is inspirational. It is no surprise that the decision was made to name a school in his honour as he is a person who can encourage youth (and all of us) to strive and build a better community, a better world.

While this book was inspired by the personal memories and stories that exist within a family, it also has a deeper meaning. Indigenous histories and stories need to be told so we all know the truth of our communities and places. It is vital that we do this to help move our country forward.

I congratulate Tom Sindlinger for the creation of this book and look forward to seeing what other projects are inspired by this work.

President, Historical Society, 2023

A MIKE MOUNTAIN HORSE
MESSAGE FOR A MODERN CANADA

His triumph was living
the beautiful image the world has of Canada:

Embrace this Canadian home,
    take it to your heart.

It is your home,
    my home,
        our home.

It is a home rich with
    magnificent mountains
        wild horses, and
            hunting hawks.

Our home represents our values:
    tolerance and respect,
    rights and responsibilities.

We share these riches and values,
    then leave a little of ourselves
        for future generations,
            just as others before
                did for us.

Embrace our Canadian home,
    take it to your heart.

And its riches and values
    will make your heart …

    Strong like a mountain …
    Spirited like a horse … and
    Soar like a hawk!

Tom Sindlinger, Kiev 1994

THE HEART AND SOUL OF A NATION

Mike Mountain Horse

c1888 - 1964

By

Mike Pisko 1938

In writing this book, it was the author's goal to emulate the approach of Mike Mountain Horse when he wrote his book:

"… it became my desire to narrate as accurately as possible some of the true facts concerning my people, <u>without exaggeration of their virtues or glossing over of their faults."</u>

INTRODUCTION: "THE DIRTY OLD INDIAN"

Mike Mountain Horse was employed as a Wiper by *Canadian Pacific Railway*. He came home from work very dirty, his traditional striped, gray railway bib-overalls covered in coal dust. His face was covered too, but it was not noticeable his skin was so dark.

He was confident and well liked by his fellow workers who elected him president of their local labour union. To celebrate his election, they took him for a celebratory beer, but he could not drink with them because it was against the law to sell alcohol to Indians.

Mike sat alone in the corner of the beer parlour, the bartender turning a blind eye because the railway workers who brought Mike in were his regular customers, and the bartender wanted their business.

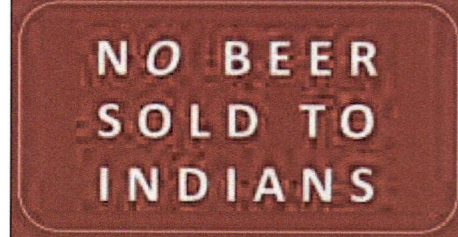

Mike took much pleasure many times describing the scene to me. Vigorously Jabbing his finger into the air, he would mimic the non-Indians in the bar who would point at him and say, "look at that dirty old Indian", that dirty old Indian being him, and every time, as though it was the first time he was telling it, he would lean back and laugh loudly.

Mike would laugh every time he told the story, because .... *he was dirty ..... he was old .... and ..... he was proud to be an Indian*. He was confident and satisfied with the things he had done. That is enough for anyone.

"The Dirty Old Indian" - what does it mean

Just 7 words in the title says more about attitudes in CANADA than thousands of words. The best thing about it is that people discuss what it means.

I have a routine when I'm asked the title. I reply the title is *"The Dirty Old Indian",* and then pause for reactions. Some react quickly, noticeably uncomfortable. I quickly add the second part of the title – MY CANADIAN HERO – and they are relieved. But the best reaction comes from Indigenous people who immediately say we get it and move on.

Non-Indigenous citizens are afraid to say much because they are afraid they will offend Indigenous. I, though, think that not talking about these things is the greater offense because we will never deal and move on.

The title, now, may be racist, but that is exactly the point. We must come to terms with this. Should the Indigenous person feel offended or should the non-Indigenous feel ashamed? My answer is neither, that's just the way it was a long time ago. Let's deal with today's reality — together.

This is where *Truth & Reconciliation* fails. *T & R* blares blame – one hand clapping. As an Indigenous friend said to me, "look at what your people have done to my people"; or the article in the *Mount Royal University* publication *Summit*, "taking back what was taken from them" and "fighting cultural appropriation" (page 64). This is adversarial, not reconciliation.

Although the title can be considered racist, almost a racial slur, it is still an accurate and contradictory portrait of history; it can make some uncomfortable reminding them of an unjust past; it is certainly challenging to compare two opposites which evoke visceral emotional responses.

But fixating on the past is missing the future.

---

[2] If this is what Mount Royal University means by "indigenizing its curriculum", the University does not meet the definition of a university as open minded and universal. It is failing its students and our country.

About the word "Indian"

Why "Indian"? Because Indians insist on living under Canadian legislation titled *The Indian Act*.

The Indian Act is a racist law. It is archaic, condescending, and patronizing and keeps Canadians and Indigenous-Canadians apart. It is a legislated barrier that separates Indians from the modern world and prevents full participation in its benefits.

> *"The native people have suffered for 130 years under a federal government policy regime that has made them wards of the state"[3].*

Indians, fearing they will lose their "fiduciary rights", have resisted any Canadian Government abolishing the *Act*. However, the Government unilaterally created the *Act*, so it can unilaterally repeal the *Act*; there is nothing to negotiate. Then Indians can be whatever they want — like Afro-Canadian, Italian-Canadian, Ukrainian-Canadian, French-Canadian, Indian-Canadian — or simply plain Canadian.

Giving Indians "First Nations" status is misleading because it implies special status, like first class, and therefore different privileges and rights; and begs the question of who was second, third, etcetera. There is no class structure in Canada.

CANADA was settled at different times by different peoples, including Indians; all seeking to improve their life, and willing to live together for the common interest. If settlers must be categorized according to when they arrived, then let it be under the *Canadian Charter of*

---

[3] MELVIN H. SMITH, *Aboriginal Land Claims in British Columbia: Serious Concerns About the Nisga'a Deal*, A Fraser Institute Occasional Paper, 1998.

> *"Melvin H. Smith, QC, spent 31 years in the public service of British Columbia ... from 1967 until 1987 he was the ranking official on constitutional law and constitutional reform issues for four successive provincial administrations. He was a key player in the patriation of the Constitution in 1981 and served as a Deputy Minister for 13 years in various ministries.... He is the author of the Canadian best-seller, Our Home or Native Land?"*

Rights and Freedoms, with the same laws and societal expectations. It is time for Indians to be Canadians.

The issue is more than the name. It is the imagery, mostly in the minds of non-Indians, behind the name. Changing the name will accomplish nothing: "a rose by any other name"[4] would smell the same. The same slang stigma associated with the name Indian will stick to the new name unless the new name earns a new image.

But it will take more than a name change to change the image. Indians will have "to walk the talk". For example, a group of young bucks, all feathers and paint and drums, entered the charity Dragon Boat races on Henderson Lake in Lethbridge. Halfway through their first sprint, they gave up, one of them vomiting over the boat's gunwales. The other three dragon boats in the sprint finished the race, all of them crewed by breast cancer survivors.

If you want to remove the stigma behind the name Indian — finish the race!

In any case, most Indians do not care what non-Indians call them, as long as it's not late for the "money dance"[5]. Just ask any young Indian boy urinating in the Elbow River just above Calgary's drinking water at the Glenmore Reservoir while laughing at Calgarians.

It is non-Indians who have the biggest problem with the word "Indian"[6]. To them, it is the connotation or social baggage the word has

---

[4] SHAKESPEARE, *Romeo and Juliet.*

[5] A dance where dancers do a "hesitation step" in a circle and the Chief walks amongst them and hands out cash.

[6] The Alberta Government is a revealing example of official confusion over what to call Indians. In 2016, the Government took the "brave" new step of changing the name of the Department of Aboriginal Relations to Department of Indigenous Relations. This "grand" gesture was no doubt done to appease the political correctness police, not because Indians were clamoring for a name change.

Before the most recent change, the Indians were referred to by the Canadian Government as Indians, or Natives, or Aboriginals, or First Nations People, or Others; and programs were designed specifically for Indian economic, social, and community projects, each of which were part of various relevant government ministries making it impossible to say just how much the Canadian Government was budgeting for them, never mind answering the question of why when Indians and their reserves are a federal creation.

accumulated over the years. A good example of the development of this image is how American movies used to portray Indians. Indians were seldom good and were in the background on horseback. John Wayne, an American movie icon, used it in at least one of his cowboy movies, by saying that "the only good Indian is a dead Indian"[7].

John Wayne had help in perpetuating the "bad Indian" image. There was the popular Saturday morning matinee idol of Hopalong Cassidy and his 50 western films, one of which has him mouthing the line "I'd have gotten a better deal from any *sidewinding half-breed* in the country"[8] (which would have had the author's half-breed mother seething and simmering) from which the listener is to assume the deal was so bad it was worse than what one could have gotten from a full-blooded Indian. Makes one wonder how bad the deal would be from a quarter breed or a "one drop" Indian.[9] In another movie, it is said that a politician's chance of being elected was improved by "wingin [shooting] Injin Joe"[10].

The "dead Indian" phrase is still with us in movies today. In 2020, in Quentin Tarantino's Best Picture Nominated Movie *Once upon a time in Hollywood*, Leonardo DiCaprio's (who was nominated for Best Actor)

To help government's difficulty in finding a contemporary, "politically correct" label for Indians, here is a suggestion: DOVES (Descendants of Original Very Early Settlers), which includes many people, Indian and non-Indian. You're welcome.

[7] . "There are 'white folk' in this country [America] to this day that still believe 'the only good Indian is a dead Indian,' a phrase which The Duke [John Wayne] helped to perpetuate." [From DANA PARSONS, columnist in the Los Angeles Times, October 9, 1994.]

The phrase was first uttered in 1869 by an American General (Sheridan) after the Civil War and reiterated by Theodore Roosevelt when speechifying before being elected President in 1901.

The Only Good Indians is a book advertised in the New York Times Book Review, December 6, 2020, page 5.

[8] Lesley Selande, Director, *Riders of the Deadline*, 1943.

[9] The one drop rule was an American practice, legal in many states, of classifying people for segregation purposes. Its primary target was Black people. One drop of blood meant that one was a Black person.

[10] *Rogue of the Range*, 1936, directed by S. Roy Luby and starring Johnny Mack Brown.

character touts the racist catchphrase 'The only good Indian is a dead Indian.'[11].

The "dead Indian" label became part of the Canadian milieu as well: "THE ONLY GOOD INDIAN: *essays by Canadian Indians*"[12] keeps the description and the undesirable and now unwanted imagery alive.

This imagery, in historical or modern terms, will be hard to erase as long as Indians are hidden away behind the Indian Curtain — *The Indian Act*. The *Indian Act* defines them legally as Indians. Want to change the name, start by abolishing *The Indian Act*.

For my part, I love my grandparents, who called themselves Indians. They evoke the modern equivalent of the romanticized *Noble Savage*. To me, Mike Mountain Horse will always be an Indian, independent, proud, and — my grandfather[13]

An essay in the New York Times academically and conclusively discusses the debate surrounding the word Indian. Judging old customs or history by today's rules:

> " makes it harder to see the complete picture, the full context; we become obsessed with obscure metrics, legalistic violations of current sensibilities. And actively changing those [words] — continually remolding them into a shape that suits today's markets — eventually compromises the entire archival record of our culture; we're left only with evidence of the present, not a document of the past. This ... leads obdurate

---

[11] THE ATLANTIC, *Quentin Tarantino's Ultimate Statement on Movie Violence*, August 2, 2019.

There is never certainty in understanding what a movie Director is trying to say, but in context, here it is more about the character who is saying it. The movie, through the character, is saying this is how mindless some people used to be a century and a half ago; and isn't it good we have moved on and recognize failures in human nature.

12 Wautageshig, New Press, 1970.

13 The cover for Mike's book Published in 1979 by the Glenbow Alberta Institute and The Blood Tribal Council, has a painting by Gerald Tailfeathers, a Blood Artist, titled "Sighting an Enemy Camp".

politicians to try and purge reams of uncomfortable ... history from textbooks, leaving students learning — and living — in a state of confusion, with something always out of order, always unexplained."

Mike's Chronology

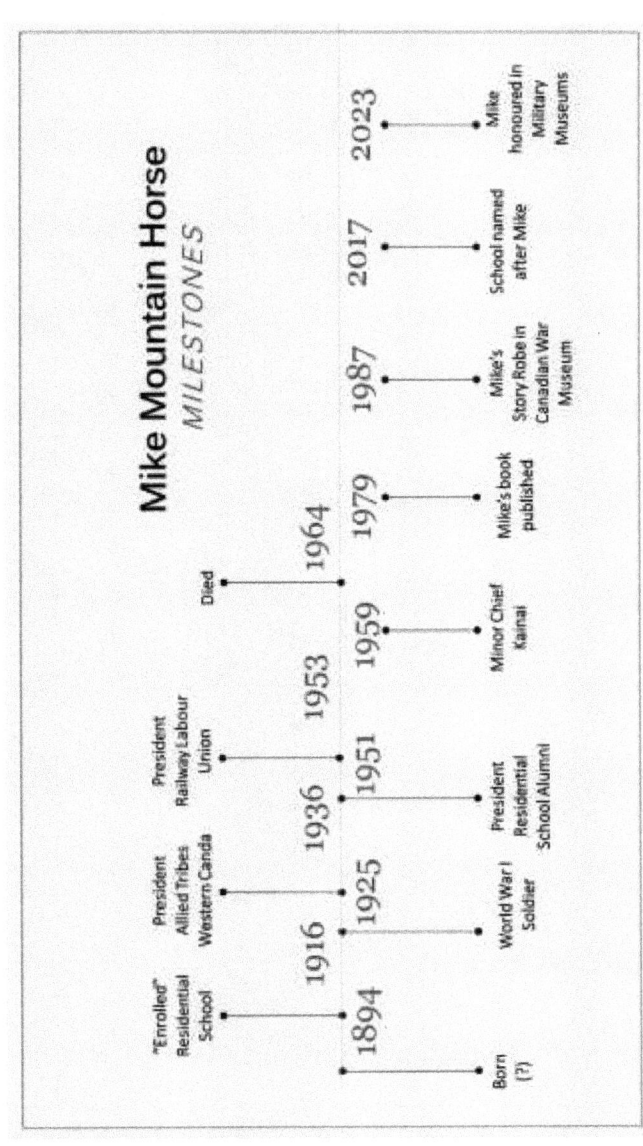

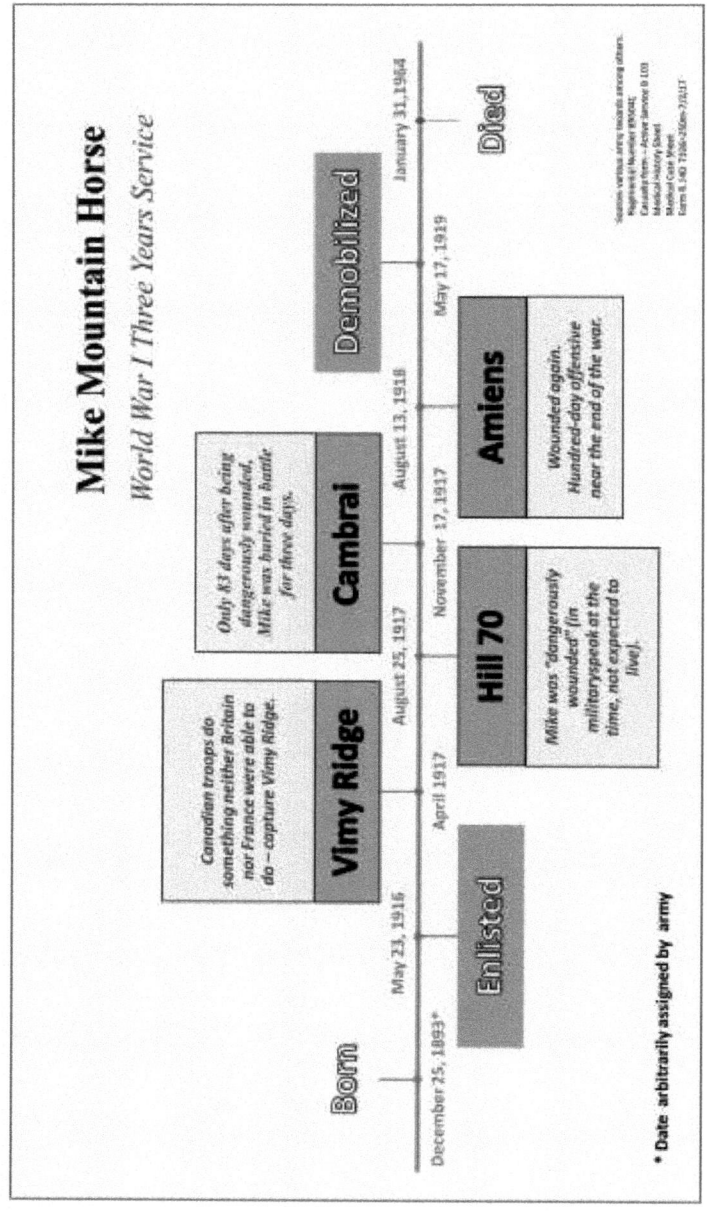

Table of Contents

List of Figures

Fiction based on Mike Mountain Horse[14]

The top half of the medal could be seen. The ribbon attached to it floated on a thin layer of urine.

In the other corner of the backyard *Siksikasomatai* (a fictitious name) was preparing a new place for the outhouse.

His name was not Benjamin Gladstone. His name was *Siksikasomatai*, as given by his mother, but the English recruiting officer could not understand this. So, like hundreds of immigration officers who did not understand new arrivals to Canada, the World War I recruiting officer arbitrarily assigned him an English name and a birth date. The officer chose Gladstone after the officer's favourite English Prime Minister, and his given name, Benjamin, after Gladstone's rival Benjamin Disraeli. *Siksikasomatai* had no idea what a birthday was, but it did not matter because his residential school did not have birthdays.

This was *Siksikasomatai's* introduction to the vagaries of non-Indian life "in a hurry". He

was no longer isolated from the real world by Reserve life — the *Indian Curtain*. The introduction was amplified by his first time on a train from the enlistment centre to the training camp in Calgary which is marked on a hillside by white-washed rocks on the southwestern edge of the City. From this hillside, the army practised lobbing shells across the Elbow River onto the Tsuut'ina Reserve. To this day, the residents of the Reserve detonate unexploded shells that rise above ground with the Spring thaw.

The young recruits at the camp, boisterously anticipating a romantic vision of wartime adventure and heroism, buddied-up and gave each other nicknames. To them, the nickname for Gladstone was obvious: "Happy Rock", but to *Siksikasomatai* it didn't mean anything, so he laughed along with his fellow recruits.

The nickname turned into a life-long wound that he deeply resented as it mocked his heritage — a resentment he never expressed until he was on his death bed.

From Calgary, *Siksikasomatai* and 1,500 other soldiers were sent by train to Montreal where they were packed into 3rd class

---

14 This fiction is the story of Mike, but it contains oral history that cannot be corroborated. Thus the fictious name.

below deck on a ship bound for South Hampton. The steamship, *Ascania,* was attacked by submarines but escaped due to its superior speed of thirteen knots over the submarine's speed of just five knots. For *Siksikasomatai*, never crowded by more than those inside his family teepee, the ocean voyage shoulder to shoulder with 1,500 other humans combined with the bone chilling fear from a simultaneous submarine attack, the voyage was a life changer. However, the horror of three years in the trenches in France would make the ocean crossing a pleasure cruise in comparison.

(On a subsequent sailing the Ascania ran aground and sank off the southwestern coast of Newfoundland. Strangely, there were no fatalities. That would be made up for in the carnage of the trenches in France.)

Siksikasomatai received three-weeks training in England before being sent to France. It gave him a chance to settle from the ocean crossing, and to be shocked by the lifestyle of the English, although given his meagre free time his exposure was limited to that around his camp, and even that was limited by his obvious ethnic difference which would leave him on the periphery. His exposure was mostly to the "camp followers" who hung around "outside the barracks by the corner

light". Nevertheless, he and his fellow Indian soldiers were favoured customers of the camp followers who were, however, disappointed by *Siksikasomatai* because he had his pay assigned to his mother in Canada.

Siksikasomatai, a full-blooded Indian, fought and was wounded three times in battles at Vimy Ridge, Hill 70, Amiens, and Cambrai. One of the wounds was categorized as "dangerously wounded", which at the time was a euphemism for "not expected to live". He was buried four days by a shell explosion.

For the first time in wars, tanks were used at Cambrai, creating mass fear in the enemy, just as Hannibal's elephants had when they were first used in battles. The tanks were an innovation implemented by Winston Churchill while he served as the Minister of Munitions. Before becoming Minister, Churchill had been First Lord of The Admiralty but was fired because of the disastrous defeat at Gallipoli that he had orchestrated despite fierce Cabinet opposition.

The trip across the channel to France was short compared to the trip across the Atlantic. It took him directly to Vimy Ridge where Canada suffered more than ten thousand casualties in taking an objective that French and British troops had several times failed to do. In preparing for the battle to take the Ridge, at different times the Canadian officers sent 60 raiding parties across no-man's-land for the purpose of gathering information, but their primary effect was terrorizing the enemy. For the enemy, the Canadians became the most feared of troops.

Much of the success of the Canadians in terrorizing the enemy was owed to the participation of Indians who would strip down and crawl into enemy trenches where they would scalp Germans, an action Canadian officers with a modicum of contrition would call "scouting". *Siksikasomatai* was one of these raiders. During his service, his knife would dispatch three enemy in hand-to-hand combat. He recorded in a post-war book that he was carrying on the "warrior tradition" of his "People" by demonstrating that they were still warriors.

Indians were segregated in a way that today is considered racist. Most, if not all, of the over four thousand Indians who served in World War I were segregated into squads rather than being integrated with all the troops, much like the Black American experience in the military until post World War II when President Truman ordered desegregation of the service. The difference between Black and Indian military discrimination was that Indians were given guns to point at the enemy. The American military was not as confident, given how Black people were treated in America, in which direction the guns would be pointed.

After the war, *Siksikasomatai* recorded his war experiences on a calf robe. Using stickman characters, the robe had twelve drawings of his battle experiences. He used this to illustrate stories he told to school children. The story most liked by children was the one where he was buried for four days by an exploding shell while on one of his night-time raids. He was in an enemy trench when one of this own shell explosions buried him. While buried, enemy soldiers would eat their rations while sitting on the debris covering him.

However, teachers, feeling the details of his war battles were too graphic for young children, would caution him. For example, children did not need to know the details of his knife struggles with enemies or that he shot others in trenches, one of them a German officer who shot him first.

The English commander asked the General of the "colonial" troops (that is Canadians, among others) to bring to their next meeting "one of those Indian fellows" he was hearing so much about. He wanted to present a

Distinguished Conduct Medal to *Siksikasomatai.*

The general, upon being introduced to *Siksikasomatai* at the medal presentation ceremony, perhaps thinking he was being friendly instead of perfunctory, flippantly asked "how ya doin chief". *Siksikasomatai* considered the greeting and its tone to be disrespectful. He instantly reacted by dropping his salute and sauntered away.

The presentation ceremony was unceremoniously ended, the medal was handed to the Canadian General who put it into his pocket to give to *Siksikasomatai* at a more agreeable time. It went through time and many pockets before going into *Siksikasomatai's* pocket when he was casually told he was now an Acting Sergeant.

After the War, *Siksikaso*matai wore the medal and his sergeant stripes on the train home where the soldiers in the car jeered him shouting "hey chief, where's your feathers?". The War over, military discipline ended, along with respect for the uniform and the Indian.

There was much respect however for *Siksikasomatai* when he returned to his Reserve. He was an honoured warrior and eventually elected a minor chief, but he had experienced modern life in the outside world, and he could not settle back into the primitive lifestyle of the Reserve. He left to live in a city, but he did not forget where he came from. It became obvious to him that his People were treated in a way which seemed to allow society to neglect the rights of Indians, especially regarding land ownership.[15] Without consulting Indians, the Canadian Government was often seen re-classifying Indian land for non-Indian use and at times selling some of the land to non-Indians.

Siksikasomatai began writing letters to editors of newspapers denouncing these practices and demanding remedial actions. The points he made in the letters were substantiated and many were of legal authority and quality in their structure and arguments.

He did not go un-noticed, but he was inherently aware that letters to the editors lasted only until the next day's newspapers. For meaningful change, Indians needed political power and that

---

[15] Indigenous Reserves do not own the land they are on. Title to the land is still with the Crown (the Canadian government). This is why Indigenous living on the Reserve can not get mortgages for houses as they don not have collateral.

meant collective action, which he organized by calling for an assembly. Over two thousand Indians from western Canada gathered at a small town close to his Reserve. There they formed *The Allied Tribes of Western Canada*; *Siksikasomatai* was its first president. The alliance eventually evolved into a modern national political lobbying force.

More than fifty-seven newspaper articles around North America noted *Siksikasomatai*'s achievement: newspapers such as the Edmonton Journal, The Province (B.C.), The Los Angeles Star, The Desert News (Salt Lake City), The Miami Herald, and The North Bay Nugget (Thunder Bay), among others.

He used his leadership abilities in his non-native community as well. At the railway where he worked, he was elected president of the local labour union. An astoundingly unique achievement for his era for an indigenous person, underline anywhere in the world underline — a minor Chief (his native society) and a labour president (his functional society)! *Siksikasomatai* succeeded in the modern world while still maintaining his cultural heritage.

Siksikasomatai was employed as wiper of railway engines that were fueled by coal. He therefore came home from work

very dirty, his traditional striped, gray-bibbed overalls covered in coal dust. Well liked by his co-workers, they invited him for a beer after they had elected him president of their union. They went across the street to a small beer parlour, but *Siksikasomatai* could not sit with them because it was against the law to sell beer to Indians. A big red sign at the entrance said, "NO BEER SOLD TO INDIANS". *Siksikasomatai* had to sit alone in a corner, the bartender turning a blind eye as the railway workers who brought *Siksikasomatai* were his regular customers, and he wanted their business.

Many times, *Siksikasomatai* took much pleasure describing the scene. Vigorously jabbing his finger into the air, he would mimic the patrons in the bar who would point and say about him, "look at that dirty old Indian", and every time as though it were the first time telling it, he would laugh loudly.

Siksikasomatai would laugh every time he told the story because … *he was dirty … he was old … and he was proud to be Indian.*

Fame however, like magnets, attracts opposites, and *Siksikasomatai* got his share. A self-styled local historian without credentials of any kind proclaimed that *Siksikasomatai* did not earn a medal. He could not find

Siksikasomatai's war records. A one-armed veteran who was a member of the *Alberta All Indian Legion* established by *Siksikasomatai* came to his defence. The veteran, a lawyer, noted that there were no records of his own service, leaving him to wonder how he had lost his arm. In the fog of war, it is a wonder any record exists for anyone, especially in the muddy morass of World War I.

The local media, however, played up the no medal story. He was shunned by his tribe. *Siksikasomatai* felt he had disgraced his people. He could also see it in the eyes of his non-Indian friends as they looked away.

Siksikasomatai, the proud Indian, was no more ....

From the window of their unpainted unheated clapboard house in the displaced persons section of town, *Siksikasomatai's* partner watched *Siksikasomatai* tip over the old outhouse and drag it to the new pit and then fill the old pit with dirt from the new one. Now the two-seater outhouse faced south, catching sunshine, and shielding occupants from the cold northerly winter winds. Next year's potatoes would grow larger because of the waste below the old outhouse, she thought, and they would be savoured by *Siksikasomatai* because of the medal buried in it.

Less than a year later, *Siksikasomatai* could see the "no-Indians" hospital across the street from the Indian hospital he was in. The divide between Indians and non-Indians lingered, as it had throughout his life, and he saw no signs of the divide ending. Indian life today, he thought, was not as good as it was 100 years ago, and unless the Indian Curtain were lifted, it would be even less 100 years in the future. Indians were an endangered species on the brink of becoming an extinct species, waiting to go extinct while hiding behind the Indian Curtain. Reservations were a dead end, as Apartheid was in South Africa. As he had written in his book, the buffalo were never coming back.

After several days languishing in a hospital bed, he said goodbye to the world. Weakly raising his wrinkled arm, the white hospital gown sliding down to his shoulder, he defiantly gestured at the "no-Indians" hospital across the street.

One week later, he was buried. To this day, his grave is unmarked.

PART I THE WAY IT WAS

"It is very easy to blame anything that doesn't work in your life on racism. But there are a lot of things that play into it. It's not quite that simple."[16]

---

[16] HUDSON, ERNIE, interview in The Independent (U.K. newspaper). Mr Hudson was the Black ghostbuster in the blockbuster international movie *"The Ghostbusters"*.

Mike confronts discrimination

This book is about a Canadian soldier and public leader's victory over racial discrimination.

On the one hand its title *"The Dirty Old Indian"* is a pejorative. Alongside this phase is MY CANADIAN HERO, which is praise.

Such a difference, how can they exist at the same time?

But they did exist at the same time for Mike Mountain Horse. What is extraordinary about this reality is how the high praise Mike earned made discrimination small and unimportant. With pride he faced down racial discrimination, his strength shining on an inspirational message. An inspiring message for Canadians because racial discrimination is still a national malaise.

Mike Mountain Horse's triumph was succeeding in non-Indian society while still retaining his Indian cultural heritage. His life shows Canadians that despite our differences, or discriminations.

Together we can live the beautiful image
the world has of CANADA.

Mike Mountain Horse - Canadian hero

1 Mike, labour president

Mike was employed as a Wiper[17] of coal-fired steam engines. He came home from work filthy, his traditional striped, gray railway bib-overalls covered in coal dust. His face was covered too, but it was not

---

[17] The Wiper's job was to work a 12-hour shift in the roundhouse, where he packed the internal moving parts of the engine with wads of greasy waste. The pay was $1.75 a day. This was the bottom rung on the ladder that rose to the train engineer's seat.

as noticeable because he was the darkest skinned Indian I ever saw, dirty or clean.

He was confident and well liked by his fellow workers. After work he went with them from the engine roundhouse to the small beer parlour[18] across the street. But he could not sit with them because it was then against the law for Indians to go into beer parlours or buy liquor.

Mike had to sit alone in the corner of the beer parlour, the bartender turning a blind eye because the railway workers who brought Mike in were his regular customers, and the bartender did not want to risk losing their business.

Mike took much pleasure describing the scene to me, many times. Vigorously Jabbing his finger into the air, he would mimic the non-Indians in the bar who would point at him and say, "look at that dirty old Indian", that dirty old Indian being him, and every time, as though it was the first time he was telling it, he would laugh loudly.

Mike would laugh loudly, every time he told the story, because .... *he was dirty .... he was old .... and he called himself an Indian.* Looking at his eyes, he was saying he was proud of himself and the things he had done. That is all you can do, and that is more than enough for anybody.

Mike Mountain Horse, before he was a "dirty, old Indian", was a scout and interpreter for the North West Mounted Police; and then

---

[18] The law at the time strictly limited liquor sales. The provincial government had a monopoly on retail liquor sales, for which the customer required a "permit"; and Indians were not allowed permits. Nor were they allowed inside beer parlours, rooms that had to be associated with hotels. The size of the parlours was related to the number of rooms in the hotel. Therefore, small hotels, small beer parlours; large hotels, large beer parlours.

The beer parlours were divided into two – one half for men, and the other half for "ladies and escorts". Women were not allowed to go alone into beer parlours.

during the First World War, he served in the *Canadian Expeditionary Force*[19], fighting at Vimy Ridge, Hill 70, Cambrai, and Amiens.

Wounded three different times, he once led a machine gun section of his battalion behind enemy defences. He was wounded[20] and buried when an exploding shell covered their shelter. It was four days before he was discovered.

He was awarded a *Distinguished Conduct Medal* for his bravery on the battlefield and at the end of the War was demobilized as an acting Sergeant[21]. If Mike had been White, he would have been an officer and awarded a medal of valour for his service, which is illustrated by his Story Robe (Page 215) in *The Military Museums* in Calgary.

---

[19] Canadian Expeditionary Force, 10th Canadian Infantry Brigade, 4th Division, 50th Battalion.

[20] Mike Mountain Horse, Dangerously wounded Page 316. Also, "Two of the stalwart Indian boys who were at Red Deer ... are reported as wounded. They belong to the Blood Reserve at Macleod and are named Mike Mountain Horse and Strangle Wolf." (Red Deer News, September 5, 1917.)

[21] L. JAMES DEMPSEY, *Alberta History 50th Anniversary Issue, A Warrior's Robe*: "he came home with battle scars, along with rank of acting sergeant ..."

VALOUR CANADA: *Connecting Canadians to Their Military Heritage.* "He received the Distinguished Conduct Medal". (http: Valour Canada.ca)

The Military Museums, Calgary, in a display case November 2021:

"Mike Mountain Horse was demobilized as an acting sergeant
and was awarded a
Distinguished Conduct Medal".

Hugh A. Dempsey, a recognized preeminent historian of Indigenous Albertans, in the introduction to My People the Bloods: "By the time he was discharged in 1918, he had reached the rank of acting sergeant and had been awarded the Distinguished Conduct Medal".

Mike missed the comradery of his fellow veterans. He used his railway pass[22] to visit veterans at the Colonel Belcher Hospital in Calgary, often taking candy to them. He also visited vets at St. Michaels Hospital in Lethbridge.

He was on the executive of the Disabled Ex-Service Men's Association.[23]

Elected president of the "first all-Indian LEGION …. Mike Mountain Horse, D.C.M."[24] The membership of the LEGION was seven *Alberta* Tribes.

Saturday mornings in the old library at the Galt Gardens in Lethbridge, he would mesmerize children with stories from his ancestors' past, or simply read stories to them. He was a spell binding storyteller.

Mike Mountain Horse Elementary School in West Lethbridge has his name in honour of the work that he did with young children. The school, however, has a picture inside its entrance and on its web site, neither of which is that of Mike.

---

[22] THE CALGARY HERALD, *"When Mike retired with a full union pension, he was the only full Indian chief employed by a railway in North America [he was] presented a pass by the Canadian Pacific Railway"*, June 15, 1953.

[23] The Lethbridge Herald, *Disabled Veterans Hold General Meeting*, November 20, 1935.

[24] THE EDMONTON JOURNAL, *Indian Vets Organize*, June 21, 1957.

MIKE MOUNTAIN HORSE

Mike Mountain Horse (Miistatisomitai), a member of the Kainai (Blood) First Nation, was born in 1888 on the Kainai Reserve in Southern Alberta. At the age of 6 Mike was sent to Anglican residential school on the Reserve.

Before the war, Mike Mountain Horse worked as a police scout and interpreter for the Royal North West Mounted Police in Fort MacLeod. Mountain Horse enlisted in May 1916 at the age of 26 after his younger brother, Albert, died on his way home from service overseas. He was one of over 4000 aboriginal soldiers to serve from Canada, also including Henry Norwest, whose story can be seen elsewhere in the museum.

Mike enlisted in the 191st Battalion, but transferred to the machine gun section of the 50th Battalion. During Mountain Horse's two years of service, he was at the battle of Vimy Ridge, Hill 70, Cambrai, and Amiens.

On 21 August 1917 during the Battle for Hill 70, Corporal Mountain Horse led the machine gun section of his battalion to an old building behind the German defences. There he secured their objective but was injured and subsequently buried alive when a German shell damaged the structure; it was 4 long days before he was discovered.

Mike Mountain Horse was demobilized as an acting sergeant and was awarded a Distinguished Conduct Medal. He also had a Kainai warrior's story robe created—both commemorate his exemplary service.

THE MILITARY MUSEUMS

Calgary, November 2021

2 Mike's war story in Military Museums

Mike was confident and well liked by his fellow workers.

Mike Mountain Horse, before he was a "dirty, old Indian", was a scout and interpreter for the North West Mounted Police; and then during the First World War, he served in the *Canadian Expeditionary Force*[25], fighting at Vimy Ridge, Hill 70, Cambrai, and Amiens.

Wounded three different times, he once led a machine gun section of his battalion behind enemy defences. He was wounded[26] and buried when an exploding shell covered their shelter. It was four days before he was discovered.

He was awarded a *Distinguished Conduct Medal* for his bravery on the battlefield and at the end of the War was demobilized as an acting Sergeant[27]. If Mike had been White, he would have been an officer and awarded a medal of valour for his service, which is illustrated by his Story Robe (Page 215) in *The Military Museums* in Calgary.

Mike missed the comradery of his fellow veterans. He used his CPR pass[28] to visit veterans at the Colonel Belcher Hospital in Calgary,

---

[25] Canadian Expeditionary Force, 10th Canadian Infantry Brigade, 4th Division, 50th Battalion.

[26] Mike Mountain Horse, Dangerously wounded Page 316. Also, "Two of the stalwart Indian boys who were at Red Deer … are reported as wounded. They belong to the Blood Reserve at Macleod and are named Mike Mountain Horse and Strangle Wolf." (Red Deer News, September 5, 1917.)

[27] L. James Dempsey, Alberta History 50th Anniversary Issue, A Warrior's Robe: "he came home with battle scars, along with rank of acting sergeant …"

Valour Canada: Connecting Canadians to Their Military Heritage. "He received the Distinguished Conduct Medal". (http: Valour Canada.ca)

The Military Museums, Calgary, in a display case November 2021:

> *"Mike Mountain Horse was demobilized as an acting sergeant and was awarded a Distinguished Conduct Medal".*

Hugh A. Dempsey, a recognized preeminent historian of Indigenous Albertans, in the introduction to My People the Bloods: "By the time he was discharged in 1918, he had reached the rank of acting sergeant and had been awarded the Distinguished Conduct Medal".

[28] When Mike retired with a full union pension, he was "the only full Indian chief employed by a railway in North America, [he was] presented a pass by the Canadian Pacific Railway." The Calgary Herald, June 15, 1953.

often taking candy to them. He also visited vets at St. Michaels Hospital in Lethbridge.

He was on the executive of the Disabled Ex-Service Men's Association.[29]

Elected president of the "first all-Indian LEGION .... Mike Mountain Horse, D.C.M."[30] The membership of the LEGION was seven *Alberta* Tribes.

Saturday mornings in the old library at the Galt Gardens in Lethbridge, he would mesmerize children with stories from his ancestors' past, or simply read stories to them. He was a spell binding storyteller.

Mike Mountain Horse Elementary School in West Lethbridge has his name in honour of the work that he did with young children. The school, however, has a picture inside its entrance and on its web site, neither of which is not that of Mike.

The southwest corner of *Alberta* is an isolated part of the world. It is blocked on the south by the American border and the sparsely settled state of Montana (the least populated state in America); on the west by the Rocky Mountains; and, by-passed on the east and north by Canada's transcontinental transportation corridor. People generally come from southwest *Alberta* rather than going there.

White people settled around Cardston when the Canadian Pacific Railway, a beneficiary of enormous federal land and resources grants, enticed Mormons from Utah to homestead, offering them free land.[31] History does not indicate if the homesteaders, the railway, or the Canadian Government noticed that Indians already lived there.

---

[29] The Lethbridge Herald, Disabled Veterans Hold General Meeting, November 20, 1935.

[30] The Edmonton Journal, Indian Vets Organize, June 21, 1957.

[31] The Mormons in Idaho had successful experience with agricultural irrigation, which the railway decided could be useful in developing the dry Palliser Triangle, of which southwestern Alberta was the extreme western part.

The Indians were named the Kainai[32], but the whites immediately renamed them the Blood. Who knows why, but the Indians could not care less what the whites called them, any more than they do now.

Mike Mountain Horse was born on the Peigan Reserve which is just north of the Kainai Reserve Mike called home. In his early twenties, he served as a scout for the Royal Northwest Mountain Police in fort Macleod. He famously tracked an escaped, alleged killer into the Porcupine Hills along the eastern slopes of the Rocky Mountains. Riding at a gallop, he abruptly stopped as the horse had overrun the trail. Backtracking, he discovered that he had rode over the escapee who was huddled in a shallow coyote burrow.

---

[32] The Kainai Reserve is the largest in Canada. It is about 1,400 kilometres square with a current population of about 3,800.

When he was twenty-six, Mike rode in a buckboard from the Blood Reserve to Fort MacLeod and joined the *Canadian Expeditionary Force* to fight in the First World War. Why he did that, I do not know, and I doubt any non-Indian ever knew. I read that he wanted to avenge his older brother[33] who died returning from the War, but that's romantic writing from a white man who knows less than I.

3 Mike Mountain Horse enlists

Mike's older brother Albert had survived three German gas attacks in Europe near Vimy. He convalesced in England after which it was determined that he was well enough to return home, which he did, as far as Montreal. His relatives on the Blood Reserve were jubilant and were planning, with the tribe, celebrations for his return within two days.

Unfortunately, Albert died in Montreal from

---

[33] Albert's "Attestation Paper", Canadian Over-Seas Expeditionary Force, No. 30396 shows his birth date as December 25, 1892; while Mike's Attestation Paper shows his birth date as November 1, 1887, which makes Mike the older brother. Albert goes on to state that his next of kin is Mrs. Mountain Horse, meaning his mother, I think, since he also states he is not married. This, plus the age discrepancy between the brothers, is either sloppy record keeping or disrespect for the two Indians enlisting, or both. Or more likely, they did not care what they told the White man.

consumption, a consequence of being gassed two times[34]. His body was returned two days later by train to MacLeod from where his warrior journey had begun, sadly met by family and tribal members, boy scouts, young cadets, and many of the people (white) of the town.[35] A

4 Crosses in Calgary, November 11, 2021

ceremony was held in the local Anglican church for which tickets had to be issued to control the large number of people expected to attend. It was still early in the War, so the local casualty rate was not yet that high. Albert, who had volunteered, was believed to be the first western Indian to do die in the First World War.

After the church ceremony in McLeod, Albert's body was carried by buckboard, teamed by one horse, to St Paul's on the reserve. Mike and two brothers sat beside the coffin in the buckboard. It was the first week in December, and one can imagine how cold it was with a prairie wind in an open buckboard for about thirty kilometers, Mike wrapped in Hudson Bay blankets, or if he was fortunate, buffalo robes. It was just as cold in their home when they reached it, it having been unoccupied and the wood burning stove unlit while they were away at the funeral. Before the horse could be watered, the ice on the water trough had to be broken, as well as the potable water inside the shanty. There was no running water, while the outhouse smell was neutralized because the contents of its pit were frozen.

---

[34] THE MCLEOD SPECTATOR NEWSPAPER, December 2, 1915, Department of Indian Affairs, Headquarters Central Registry System: First Series: C-8510 "… this gallant boy who gave his life willingly for his King and Empire, although not called upon to do so." I doubt that Albert knew what the Empire was, and he probably cared even less.

[35] Albert's name is inscribed on the cenotaph in Fort McLeod.

Five months later, now in the Spring with new purple prairie crocuses and yellow buffalo beans[36] making the trip appear festive, Mike rode in the back of the same buckboard back to McLeod where he enlisted, along with his bother Joe who was sitting beside him. The prairie flowers may have been festive, but one can imagine how Mike's

mother, Sikski, felt having already lost one son, Albert, in the War and now two others were leaving to fight[37].

Mike's mother believed that Albert's enlistment was a result of encouragement from Reverend Samuel Henry Middleton, the principal of St Paul's residential school, and therefore *Alberta*'s death was on the Reverend. For two weeks she went to "Middleton's house seeking vengeance ..... [at one point the] grieving mother attacked Middleton with a knife and might have killed him if another of her sons had not intervened".[38]

From Fort McLeod, he went by train to Calgary for training just below Signal Hill where today there is a memorial to those who trained there. Then to Montreal and ship to England. The culture shocks this Indian from southwest *Alberta*, a dry isolated corner of the world, went through must have been of earthquake size. But that shock was nothing compared to the shock to come in the trenches of World War One.

---

[36] Picture by Bob Sindlinger who can be seen in Calgary as a child with his grandmother Mary Mountain Horse on page 38.

[37] The award-winning movie Saving Private Ryan, starring Tom Hanks in 1999, was about the American Army's response to the loss of three brothers in the Second World War.

[38] JAMES DEMPSEY, "Mountain Horse, Albert", in Dictionary of Canadian Biography, vol. 14, University of Toronto. http:www.biographi.ca/en/bio/mountain_horse_albert_14E.html

In a letter to Middleton, Albert said that he was "going forth to fight for King and country". Such a comment, although it might have been meaningful then, is laughable now, regardless of whether one is Indian or non-Indian.

Wounded three different times, once "Dangerously Wounded"[39], he fought at Vimy Ridge, Hill 70, Cambrai, and Amiens. He led a machine gun section of his battalion[40] behind enemy defenses. He was wounded and buried when an enemy shell demolished their shelter. It was four days before he was discovered. During the time he was buried, a German soldier ate his lunch while sitting on the debris that covered Mike.

Mike Mountain Horse was awarded a *Distinguished Conduct Medal* for his bravery on the battlefield and at the end of the War was demobilized as an Acting Sergeant.

After the War, he worked for the Canadian Pacific Railway until retiring with a union pension, which combined with his Treaty money, made him one of the wealthiest Indians from the Blood reserve. During his years at the railway, he walked to and from work. He did not drive and there was not bus service.

Between his work and home was flat open prairie with a narrow twenty-meter-wide gulley in the middle. Rattlesnake Gulch he called it. If a snake wanted to shake your hand he said, first chew some prairie grass and then rub it on your hand. Then the snake would not bite you. What five-year-old would not believe that.

His home was in an outlying area of Lethbridge called *Number Three* (after a nearby coal mine shaft) by city officials, but local residents called it DP. DP stood for Displaced Persons who were people from Europe displaced by war.

---

[39] Dangerously wounded, page 313.

[40] CANADIAN EXPEDITIONARY FORCE, 50th Battalion, Mike Mountain Horse, Form R. 149, 7106 – 25 Om – 7/2/17.

Alcohol in *Alberta* was a government monopoly. People, even non-Indian, needed a "Permit" (pronounced "per mitt") to buy liquor.[41] My dad, who was white, had a Permit, which made it very convenient for Mike's friends (Mike did not drink or smoke). It also helped that my

5 *Bootlegger for Mike's friends*
(also the author's parents)

Dad worked at the Lethbridge brewery, so beer supply was not a problem.[42]

Mike spent two years of his youth in a church operated government funded "residential school". The purpose of these residential schools was to assimilate Indians into non-Indian society. Whether or

---

[41] Alberta's Government was Social Credit, a bible-first political Party that in an attempt to legislate morality had very strict and prohibitive laws.

[42] As well as a bootlegger, my Dad was a cattle rustler, but he said they did not keep him in jail more than a night for that. He also ran booze to the U.S. border during prohibition. They would load one of five different trucks and then "scatter and drive like hell out of Lethbridge". The Canadian police were so understaffed, they did not bother to try and follow them.

not the Indians of the time wanted to be assimilated, I do not know. Modern Indians say the assimilation was forced, an attempt to oblite-rate their culture, especially their language.

Learning a common language or how to function in a complex so-ciety was probably a good idea. Those who do not adapt to changes suffer. For example, Chief Small Boy, a Cree Indian, said to hell with the white man's evil ways, and in 1968 led over a hundred Indians into the bush in west-central *Alberta* where they set up teepees. Of course, they had to use white men's trucks to drive into town for groceries at white men's stores using money given them by the white man's government; and then when autumn nights became chilly, for white men's propane heaters and propane. When winter came, Chief Small Boy decided that practical matters were paramount to the desire for the "old ways" of doing things. Eventually, they returned to the reserve in order to receive royalties from oil development.

However, notwithstanding any benefits that may have come from residential schools, most modern Indians maintain that their an-cestors and subsequently their descendants (that is themselves) are "survivors"[43] from the residential schools; and consequently, should be

---

[43] The word "survivor" has many different connotations, invoking meaning beyond a word's intended meaning. Surviving could mean making a school team, maintaining a business through a recession, living through a tragedy, or defying World War II's death camps, among others. Surviving the Holocaust is at the pinnacle of surviving, the ulti-mate triumph of good over evil. Being at Indian residential school comes nowhere near the sacrifice, suffering, and evil in the Nazi death camps.

Branding residential school youth as survivors is hyperbole that undermines the atten-tion the residential school issue deserves. In political terms, the exaggeration creates more public push back than support.

There is enough documented evidence around to reveal the deplorable conditions en-dured by some residential school "inmates". Being ripped away from your parents when you are 6 years old; forced to speak another language and punished if you did not; and being physically and sexually abused, is unpardonable.

Not all residential schools abused or mistreated their charges, but there is not one resi-dential school in this or any other country that can justify separating children from their parents.

Inmates is not a misnomer when referring to children in residential schools. Inmates is what they were: they were hunted down and returned to the school if they tried to find their way home.

Indians have been affected by their parents/grandparent's incarceration in residential schools. They never experienced what it was like to be in a family, they couldn't observe,

monetarily compensated. So the Government compensated them[44]. The payments were intended to help Indians recover from the emotional and physical abuse they allege occurred in the residential schools. I don't know how money erases bad memories, but as a senior bureaucrat in Ottawa said to me once, "Indians think they can come to Ottawa and get money any time they want. And they think this because they get it".

Mike attended residential school[45]. Near the end of his life he was a leader in his community. He was a an honorary chief and in his white community a school in Lethbridge is named after him. Mike and Mary Mountain Horse successfully parented five children, three of whom served during World War II. My Mother was in residential school and off the reserve successfully raised five children. Two of my aunts served in the Canadian forces during World War II. One aunt was at a residential school for eight years. She became a registered nurse. I asked her about abuse at the residential schools. Her answer was "The only abuse I saw was Indians abusing Indians".

Indians refer to those Indians, and their descendants, who went to residential school as "survivors", who have been traumatized forever. Sorry, but those who survived the Nazi death camps were survivors. Compared to these people, not much can be said about the Indians' on reserves

---

learn or experience parenting skills, some parents turned to alcohol or drugs in bereavement for their lost children and they in turn have done the same and are still a lost generation.

It will be a few more generations before Canada's first prime minister sees his dream of assimilation realized. What would our society look like today had he not chosen the Indian Act, reservations and residential schools as a way of assimilation. It would be nice if all people could have a good long look at both sides of a sad and sorry part of Canadian history.

[44] Every Indian "survivor", or their descents, who attended a residential school received $10,000 for the first year of schooling and $3,000 for each subsequent year from a fund of about $2 billion (Canada, Indian Residential Schools Settlement Agreement).

Compare this to the what the combat soldiers got who were actual survivors in two world wars —NOTHING!

[45] Mike's classmate was Senator James Gladstone, Canada's first Treaty Indian in the Senate.

Yet listening to CBC Radio recently, there was an Indian caller complaining that her daughter had not received a share of the compensation Indians received for being in residential schools. After all, she railed on, the caller's grandfather had attended residential school and the emotional impact on him was handed down to her and through her to her daughter. Really?

This is not an unusual case. It is manifested in a much too common sense of entitlement. One senior Indian explained it to me as a "fiduciary right". I had to look that up. Simply, it is the Crown's (Government) obligation to a third party (Indigenous peoples). Indians generally maintain the Crown was negligent in this obligation, and they sue the Crown in any imaginable way their non-Indian consultants can contrive, regardless of the plausibility. The obstruction[46] of the Trans Mountain Pipeline is a current example of how this fiduciary right is bandied. Indigenous people complain that they have not been adequately consulted about the construction of the pipeline. The Government and the oil[47] companies consult intensively and extensively but get nowhere. In the end, the meaning of the word consultation[48] means, to the pipeline companies, let's compromise; to the Indians, it means more "cash".

---

[46] In a 1949 movie (*Canadian Pacific*, starring Randolph Scott and Jane Wyatt, both of whom stayed with her husband future American President Ronald Regan at the *Banff Springs Hotel*) a tactic was used to stop the construction in 1880 of Canada's railway from Calgary to Vancouver that was similar to the tactic used in 2020 to stop the construction of the *Trans Mountain Pipeline*.

In the movie, the owner of trading posts between Calgary and Vancouver would lose his fur trading business if the railway were built. In order to stop the railway being built, he enlisted the Indians: "I've thought up a new thing that will stop the railway. The railway is as good as stopped. Pass me that jug. I'm going up to talk to the Indians. Come Spring, we'll have every Tribe between here and Vancouver beating the war drums. A big uprising will end it [that is, the railway]."

[47] The word oil is used throughout to include natural gas and all petroleum by-products, such as propane, butane, condensate, etcetera.

When searching for oil, geologists do not know if they will find oil or gas, and indeed, they often find both associated. In the early days of oil exploration, drillers were very disappointed if they found a gas field instead of an oil field. However, in later years as the oil industry matured, explorers and governments had years when gas revenues exceeded oil revenues.

[48] Indians generally do not have any relevant expertise (economic, financial, technical, operational, environmental, etcetera) to contribute to consultations. It basically boils down to how much their non-Indian consultants, who are funded by the Canadian

The Trans Mountain Pipeline expansion was twice approved by the Canadian Government, but its construction was set back by court challenges by the British Columbia Government and indigenous groups. The B.C. Government maintained that it could regulate (that is, tax) what flowed through the pipeline, which was so clearly a federal government authority in regard to interprovincial commerce, that B.C.'s resistance was purely incompetent political posturing. The Supreme Court was not swayed. However, the B.C. Government was.[49]

It is always difficult to determine what Indians want, but generally they have fallen back on the plaintive plea that they were not "consulted". A Supreme Court, not wanting to be accused of discrimination against Canada's long discriminated group, agreed. After the first government approval of the pipeline, the Supreme Court ruled that the pipeline proponents must do more consultation. They did, and there were still those who said they had not been consulted. This time the Supreme Court said enough and approved the pipeline.

However, after the final Supreme Court approval of the pipeline, three indigenous groups "vowed the pipeline will never be finished"[50]. This despite "that of 129 indigenous groups invited to participate in the consultation process, more than 120 either supported the project or did not oppose it"[51].

---

government, tell them, under the guise of consultation, how much they can hold out for before a private oil company will walk away. It is like an insurance company calculating a limit up to which they will pay a claim, and after which they will go to litigation.

[49] In order to move the pipeline construction along, the oil companies wrote the B.C Government a $2 billion dollar cheque. The B.C. Government had held up the pipeline because of the Government's unbendable concern about harming the environment. This despite the fact the new pipeline was being built along the same route of an original pipeline that had operated without harm for over half a century. Such was the B.C. Government's righteous concern about the environment – save the environment unless you pay us.

[50] The Calgary Sun, Appeal Dismissed, July 3, 2020.

[51] The Calgary Sun, Kenny applauds top court decision, July 3, 2020

Consultation is a cottage industry for many Indians. It means that as many as can, whether interested or not, be consulted, which means they are paid travel, food, hotel, and a per diem of several hundred dollars. The more consultations, the more per diems. These per diems and all the costs and expenses for the legal challenges come from the taxpayer to fight a taxpayer approved project. A little irony there.

The frivolous and spurious obstruction of the Trans Mountain construction lost about four revenue earning years, "the project's delay costing Canadians $40 million every day"[52], or $58 billion (which equals over $2,000 for every Canadian who filed taxes in 2019) ..... for "consultation with Indians".

---

[52] CTV Edmonton, Trans Mountain delays costs $40 million a day: Alberta Government, September 13, 2018.

James Gladstone - Canadian Senator

James Gladstone is touted as Canada's first "Treaty Indian" Senator. A Treaty Indian is a person who belongs to a band[53] that has signed a treaty with the Canadian Government. He was at residential school on the reserve with Mike Mountain Horse.

He married my grandmother's sister, Janie. You can see a picture of Senator James Gladstone on the ten-dollar bill (he is the guy on the right). He ended up on the currency because he was CANADA's first senator from a treaty First Nation.

6 Canada's first Treaty Indian Senator

Canadian Senators are not elected, they are arbitrarily appointed by the Prime Minister and are tenured until age 75. Their appointments are based on contributions of service and money to the Party of the Prime Minister; or, the personal whim of the Prime Minister. In any case, the potential appointee must make themselves known to the Party system and become of use to the Party in its quest for and holding of power.

---

[53] An Indian band is defined as a body of Indians for whose collective use and benefit lands have been set apart or money is held by the Crown, or who have been declared to be a band for the purpose of the Indian Act. Many Indian bands have elected to call themselves a First Nation and have changed their band name to reflect this. With the 1985 amendment to the Indian Act of Canada (Bill C-31), many Indian bands exercised the right to establish their own membership code, whereby it was not always necessary for a band member to be a Registered Indian according to the Indian Act. [Statistics Canada, Data Tables, 2016.]

I have no idea, and I doubt anyone ever had, how James Gladstone got an appointment to the Senate. I surmise that the appointment of a Treaty Indian gave the Party bragging rights: "Look we are so broad minded and inclusive we have an Indian in our Senate", the same as a modern Party bragging it has a Black or a woman in it.

Now, I played with Senator Gladstone's grandson Jimmy because the Senator's wife Janie, was my great aunt.

Jimmy Gladstone - World Calf Roping Champion

Our teammates called him "Happy Rock". We played basketball together. When we were younger, we played together at his grandfather's ranch.

The first I remember of Jimmy was at the *Calgary Stampede*. We were little kids, left to run around the *Indian Village*, which then was a collection of teepees just inside the main gate. The green grass had been trampled so much that in the moist earth it looked like shell fossils.

James, or Jimmy as we called him, went on to become a *World Champion Calf Roper*. His dad Fred told him to only rodeo in a timed event because in a judged event the Indian would always be judged lower than the cowboy.

7 Jimmy Gladstone
World Calf Roping Champion

So, Jimmy became a calf roper, a timed event. I remember him training young Indians to rope. "Flank 'em", he would yell, "don't dance with em, flank em" (that is, grabbing the calf by the leg and trying to throw it down instead of grabbing the calf by its side and throwing it down). To demonstrate he jumped onto his horse and chased down a calf, which was certain about what it wanted to do, and it wanted to dance. I laughed loudly at Jimmy as he struggled with the calf and I yelled: "flank em Jimmy, flank em".

Years later, we were playing a basketball game in Calgary. My infant son Grady was there. I don't know what Jimmy, with his big smile and laughter, was thinking - calf or what - but he picked up my three-year-old son Grady by the arms and threw him into the air above his head, and Jimmy was six feet tall. I was shocked, seeing my young son flailing so high above. Fortunately, Jimmy had good hands, and if he had been on a football team, he would have been on the "good hands" squad; or as a rodeo cowboy in the event that did require good hands – calf roping.

One year, Jimmy was only seconds away from winning the calf roping championships at the Calgary Stampede. He was the leading roper, last to rope for the grand prize. He tied down his calf with a winning time. He returned to his horse. The arena judge held his red flag up for the five seconds the calf had to remain tied. If the calf got up before that time was up, it was no time for the roper, and he lost. Jimmy sat on his horse and watched the calf. Half a second to the end of time, the calf broke the rope and jumped up. The arena judge dropped his flag and Jimmy was disqualified.

The judge was his dad Fred.

His sister Connie said nobody saw Jimmy for weeks.

But Jimmy came back. He came back to be the Canadian calf roping champion three times; the world championship in 1977; and Calgary Stampede Guy Weadick award recipient in 1978. Of course, he is in the *Alberta Sports Hall of Fame*, as well as the *Pro Rodeo Hall of Fame*.

The Weadick award is presented annually to one "who best embodies what the cowboy stands for, and who best typifies the spirit of the Calgary Stampede. It is based upon ability, appearance, showmanship, character, sportsmanship and cooperation with other cowboys, the arena crew, the media and the public."

He was called to the *Alberta* Bar in 2001.

However, for all he achieved, something was missing. I always saw it in his eyes, but I did not really understand it until he phoned one morning and asked me to his wedding reception that evening at the Westin Hotel in Calgary. I did not know he was getting married and would not have expected an invitation. But the reception was that evening, and could I please come. Knowing I was just an afterthought but not why, I said sure.

Everyone was seated when I arrived. There were about twelve tables for guests, and not wanting to walk in front of everyone, I sat at the first open spot I saw. Looking around the room, it suddenly occurred why I had been asked to attend. Every table was occupied by Indians. I was at the only white table. I felt terrible.

He was caught between his Indian heritage and his rodeo non-Indians, who drew a very distinct line between cowboys and Indians. He cherished his Indian heritage, but he wanted the respect of his rodeo and legal community. He did not feel he had either when he was being derided with the moniker "Happy Rock". And even if he was not called that, he felt that everyone saw him as the Indian in the room.

Joking with him about the benefits he got from his preferential Indian status, I asked him how, because we were equally Indian, how I could get on the Band List and thus get equal Indian benefits. "Easy", he said, "you have to be voted on".

"By whom" I asked.

With the blandest expression he said, "by about two thousand Indians". In other words, you do not have a hope in hell.

Whenever I had a chance, I always referred to him as my "Cousin Jimmy".

Chief Big Plume - Warrior

8 Sandford Big Plume Former Treaty 7 Chief

"We're warriors."

Sandford Big Plume is a visionary. Raising and sweeping his arm, he pointed here and there and described what he saw as development potential on the northeast corner of his *Tsuu T'ina Reserve*. The corner was firmly embedded in the southwest corner of Calgary, its natural foothills beauty standing out from the big city development surrounding it. From a developer's viewpoint, it was a gold mine. It was the way the west used to be, still untrammeled by settlement.

But I knew Sandford was right — define your own future in a world that would not in the long term leave you alone:

> *"We talk about conciliation; we talk about the residential school and all that. There's going to have to come a point in time where we're going to have to say put that aside, enoughs enough; we gotta get on with it, we're warriors. We're First Nations people, we know how to live but having that scar on us, we gotta make a deal. I understand it will take time, but my kids my grandkids, we gotta grow up, we gotta get on with life here. We can't sit back ....."[54]*

---

[54] NATIONTALK, March 6, 2017, Sandford Big Plume, General Manager, Community Futures Treaty Seven. http://nationtalk.ca/story/sandford-big-plume-general-manager-community-futures-treaty-seven

This is a brave new attitude, and simply by saying this, he is acknowledging the entitlement Indians feel, always hiding behind their "fiduciary rights", demanding more while doing little to earn more. He is brave in saying this because he is focusing on the problem ,not the symptoms, knowing most Indians would not agree with him.

In calling for Indians to get on with life, young Indians in particular — "we are warriors" — he is saying the old way of doing things are over. It is a new world, white, black or red, be proud of yourself and the things that you can do. It is up to you.

So c'mon Warriors. Walk the talk. Be a Sandford Big Plume.

Charles Barkley - Racism as a crutch

"The Black and Hispanic communities are more vulnerable to Covid-19 because of economic and systematic discrimination. But what that comes down to is education and the type of job you have. Make sure you get an education, use the system so the system doesn't use you ...

"I hate using the term systematic racism because it gives people a crutch. We have to accept the fact that there is systematic racism, but that does not give you an excuse for failure. We can't go back and worry about history; it is what it is, we are what we are ...

"At the end of the day, it's all going to come down to personal responsibility. We can't fail and then say it's because of systematic racism; the system made me fail."[55]

9 Charles Barkley tells it like it is

These words are from a television interview of a famous former Black professional basketball player in THE UNITED STATES. He was selected as one of the top 50 players of all time and continued in basketball as a regular television analyst. During this time, he earned a reputation as being frank and outspoken. His remarks throughout his career about discrimination were respectfully considered by some Whites and fervently supported by most Blacks.

The interview was conducted by two erudite Black men, both of whom were regular anchors on CNN and were younger than Mr Barkley, and was intended to discuss the predominantly large majority of Blacks and Hispanics who had caught and died from the Covid-19 virus. The question was how come?

---

[55] CNN, *The Color of Covid*, interview of Charles Barkley, April 18, 2020.

What Barkley says here is a lot like what Chief Sandford Big Plume says on page 56.

Generally, the conclusion was because of poverty. The two large subcultures of American society, Black and Hispanic, together accounting for almost a third of the total population, mostly lived in crowded conditions because they could not afford anything with more space. Proximity made transmission of the virus easier. At the peak of the Covid-19 world-wide pandemic, the only defense was known as "social distancing". Social distancing meant staying 2 meters apart and staying home.

People living in poverty did not have the luxury of staying home, they needed whatever minimum wage they could earn; and, they did not have spacious homes anyway.

From the conclusion that poverty was the origin of the problem, the question was why they were poor[56], and the general agreement was that education was not pursued as much as it was by Whites who therefore got the better jobs and higher income. This led to the discussion of two phrases: the first was "systemic discrimination" and the second was "racial discrimination", which prompted the above comments by Mr Barkley.

Mr Barkley's comments face reality and provide valuable advice. Making them even more significant is their universality. The words Blacks and Hispanics could easily be replaced by the word Indian and still be as germane.

For example, Mount Royal University (MRU), located in Calgary and contiguous to the Tsuu T'ina Nation, twice a year publishes a magazine titled *Summit*. Its primary purpose is to maintain contact with alumna and their money. The Spring/Summer 2020 issue had an article in which two of the headers in the article reveal the head-in-the sand points of view of far too many indigenous initiatives.

The headers are:

"Taking back what was taken from them, and

---

[56] I recall some time long ago and immediately forgotten $5 million research project in The United States, the goal of which was to find out why people were poor. With a straight face, their final report concluded "people were poor because they didn't have any money".

Fighting cultural appropriation[57]

Neither of these deal with needs of students; that is, the future. They are a focus on history and getting back at those who are non-Indian, that is those who took something undefined and, in most cases, subjective. Their basic solution is for the law to be amended to provide protection of indigenous intellectual property, which they define as unique identities, land-based stories, and industrial designs and intellectual property rights. If there are to be laws for indigenous people because they are unique, then there would have to be laws for Ukrainians and Italians and Hutterites and Moslems, also unique.

The article manages to place 21 pictures of Indians on its two pages, each taking a defiant pose, not a smile among them. An aside is given to the outcome of special status, that is "entitlement ..... and how it works to dehumanize Indigenous People and cultures, not just historically but contemporarily". To define entitlement, they could start by examining how many of them qualified for MRU (that is, graduated from high school); worked and saved over summer to pay for their tuition; were working after school and weekends to pay rent and buy food; and graduated (that is, attended classes, completed assignments, passed exams) from the courses in which they were enrolled. Next time they are in the cafeteria eating a hamburger paid for by the Canadian government, they could say thank you to the non-Indian taxpayer beside them who paid for their hamburger.

Appropriating their culture?. Who would want to when the most that is seen of it are inebriated Indians on the C Train or passed out in the atrium at City Hall; or blockading railroads and the Canadian economy or demanding cash payments for every historical accusation, real or imagined? On the other hand, however, who would not want to appropriate every cultural characteristic of a Mike Mountain Horse. When more Mikes are seen, there will be fewer questions of how much is the gross economic product on a reserve; or what is the reserve's contribution to gross provincial product; or, what are the reserves' contribution to Canadian Gross Domestic Product. At this time, many non-Indians would say that Indians take far more out than they put in. It is time to put up or shut up.

---

[57] Summit Spring/Simmer 2020, Otahpiaaki, page 26.

For comparison purposes, *Alberta* Hutterite[58] colonies have lived a communal form of life for over a 100 years within the Canadian context while retaining their dress, customs, and language.[59] In 2016, there were 180 colonies in *Alberta* with about 16,000 occupants who produced 80% of *Alberta*'s eggs[60], 33% of *Alberta*'s hogs, over 10% of *Alberta*'s milk.[61]

I cannot find any similar information on *Alberta*'s 140 reserves[62] or the 120,000 "First Nations" people[63] on them.

How the Hutterites contribution to *Alberta*'s economy was made without any government or grants or subsidies is a mystery, to some. The colonies are independent but compliant with Canadian law. Perhaps Indians could be similar contributors to Canada with the Hutterite model of self-sufficiency.

Older Indians lament that they are losing, for whatever reason, if they have not lost already, their language, their culture. Younger Indians hide behind the lamentation to shield themselves from anything that demands personal responsibility or accountability. For example, a young Indian I know was shot and seriously wounded by his wife. In her defense in Calgary court, she argued that this was an Indian cultural matter, something that could not be understood by another culture, that is non-Indian. The foolish judge agreed and sentenced the accused to an "Indian Sentencing Circle"[64], and you can guess what became of that.

---

[58] Hutterites are descendants of a religious group of Germans who immigrated via Russia to The United States. Facing discrimination there during the First World War, many of them migrated to Western CANADA.

[59] RYAN, JOHN, Hutterites in CANADA, July 2013.

[60] A friend notes that chickens might argue about who produced those eggs.

[61] EVANS, SIMON, Adjunct Professor University of Calgary, *Exploring Alberta's* Past 'The Arrival of the Hutterites in Alberta'.

[62] ALBERTA GOVERNMENT, *Facts About Aboriginal People in* Alberta, July 2014.

[63] STATISTICS CANADA, Aboriginal Peoples: Fact Sheet for Alberta, March 2016. https://www150.statcan.gc.ca/n1/pub/89-656-x/89-656-x2016010-eng.htm

[64] This is not unlike Muslims asking for Sharia law instead of Canadian law to be used when Muslims are involved, which as a precedent would mean that any group could be allowed to have their law, whatever it might be, applied whenever they wanted, or whenever they perceived a benefit. I can see it now, hockey players invoking hockey law, as when some player in amateur hockey and her father (yes, Indian) in Lethbridge recently violently attacked a referee.

10 Mary Mountain Horse and author's brother

Mr Bean - The "new intolerance"

Reading was always a pleasure, until high school when what had been an adventure or just a good read, the meaning of a book was explained by a teacher, and I was sure that I had read the wrong book.

For example, the *Last of the Mohicans*. On the hero, or protagonist side of the story, was Hawkeye[65], a White guy and his two Indian sidekicks, both of whom in the 1937 movie version of the book were White, but that did not matter, it was a movie after all. Shakespeare had men and boys playing women's roles, so it did not matter who played Indians, or Chinese, or whatever, they were only actors and if they succeed in suspending our disbelief, goal accomplished.

I was at a play in a Bangkok Hotel. When it finished, there was a short popcorn intermission and then the play was started over again, but with all the players assuming opposite roles, men or women or whatever. The second version of the play was as good as the first, and although all I could do was count money from one to ten in Thai, I enjoyed both versions. So, let's get over the angst about "cultural appropriation" just because the actor portraying a character is not the same ethnicity as the character. If an actor must be the same as the character, then it would follow that a murderer must play the role of a character who is a murderer. How would that go over?

The classroom explanation of *Last of the Mohicans* describes the book as multi layered, about colonialism and anti-colonialism; and interracial marriage (that's a euphemistic referral to the relationship between an Indian and a non-Indian, so that the teacher did not have to say an Indian was boinking a White woman, or vice versa); and discrimination (English versus French and German mercenaries; and imperialists versus colonialists, and vice versus; and Whites versus Indians and Indians versus Indians and Whites).

There are three different movie versions of the book. I liked the version with Randolph Scott as Hawkeye because Randolph was a scratch golfer; and when humans got shot or scalped or stuck with an arrow in the movie they just quietly laid down and let the scene continue around them. No blood or guts or gore.

---

[65] Hawkeye is the Indian origin of the nickname for Dr Pierce in the long running television series *Mash*.

The modern version with Daniel Day Lewis was great because of the sweeping, rolling music and the running through the forest that I used to love doing naked. But the close-up, no details overlooked, of Magua holding the still beating, bleeding heart of the British Colonel was too much for me. Now, some activists would complain that it was discrimination because the gross act was committed by an Indian, but that reminds me of the scene in Mel Gibson's movie the *Patriot* where the British Captain locks colonial women and children in a church and burns it to the fucking ground.

So, which dude was worse, the Indian or the white Captain? [66]

A famous Economist wrote a book titled *"There is no such thing as a free lunch."*[67] He meant that in order to get one thing, another must be given up, which has evolved into a tenet of Economics — opportunity costs.

However, this was not the origin of the free lunch phrase. It has been used to describe, among other things, physics — the universe is a

---

[66] Wes Studi is the name of the Oklahoman actor playing Magua in this version of the movie. He is a real Indian as compared to the non-Indians in the other versions of *Last of the Mohicans*, among many others. More than the stomach-turning image of the Colonel's still pumping heart held high in his hand was the primeval fear permeating my body by the ferocity in Studi's face, his acting being so powerful.

Notwithstanding his acting skills and his stellar characterization of Magua, Studi had difficulty getting roles other than portraying an Indian, a stereotyping he lamented by referring to his acting career as one of "leathers and feathers" (The New York Times, Wes Studi, November 29, 2020. "... directors like to use his face as a blunt symbol of the Native American experience, as a mask of nobility, of suffering. Of pain that's unknowable ...).

I guess in Hollywood it was easier to make-up a white person to look like an Indian than vice versa. Canadian Indian award winners who have had success playing Indians come to mind: Chief Dan George (Little Big Man, 1970); Graham Greene (Dances With Wolves, 1990); Adam Beach (Windtalkers, 2002); Eugene Brave Rock (Wonder Woman, 2017. Brave Rock is from Mike's Kainai Reserve. Brave Rock researched Mike's war history to prepare for this role.); and, Tantoo Cardinal (Legends of the Fall, 1994).

[67] Milton Freidman, 1976 Nobel Memorial Prize in Economic Sciences, *There's No Such Thing as a Free Lunch,* 1975.

closed system in which its total being will remain forever the same, (however long that is; or if it is not too long, we will wait forever[68]) in one form or another, regardless of changes. In environmental speak, it means there are consequences to everything (like, if a butterfly moves its wings in JAPAN it will play a part in a tornado in Texas; or one small change in the present can change the whole future). In social terms, it means that benefits from government for one group will have draw-backs for another group.

Generally, there is nothing to which the phrase does not pertain, in one way or another. In politics, political promises are always free without regard to cost or merit. In politics, as opposed to government, the phrase "there is no such thing as a free lunch" may, without much hesitation, be associated with anything and everything, anytime.

Politics is concerned solely with getting elected, and then re-elected, and to accomplish that, promises are the only currency the pol-itician has, and to enhance the promise it is implied, if not directly stated, that those to whom the promises are being made, will be getting something for free if they vote for the promiser. One way or another, if the promiser is elected to the government and the promises are acted upon by the government, these promises will have a cost in terms of the resources and sanctions needed to realize them and the alternate choices displaced.

This brings us to Mr Bean's discussion of the meaning of free speech[69] and the use of the word Indian and the controversy of the sub-ject given our liberal attitude in a relatively free society. First, there is the struggle with the word free – what does it mean. Does it mean that there is no cost to it; does it mean the cost is the alternative? Colloqui-ally, we assume that anything goes that does not cause harm, like the potential harm from yelling "fire" in a crowded theatre. But what is the harm, and to whom, if a campaigning politician refuses to kiss a baby with a disagreeable odour? The baby probably is indifferent while the mother might be offended. So it would seem that in this case, no direct harm no foul; it is simply a form of free speech.

---

[68] Oscar Wilde (kind of), *The Importance of Being Earnest*, 1894. The actual quote is "If you are not too long, I will wait here for you all my life".
[69] https://www.youtube.com/watch?v=BiqDZlAZygU

But what about the mother's feelings. Is she offended, and should there be a penalty for offending her? Who defines harm, and the penalty for harming? Are there levels of harm that require a comparative response from society? Are there levels that should be free from consequence, or sanctioned, or ignored, like calling one a "dirty, old Indian"?

Alberta had a modern (1985) court case that in a general way dealt with these questions. The case attracted global interest. A public-school teacher and small-town mayor, James Keegstra, in Eckville (population of about 700 at the time, located southeast of Edmonton) was accused of inciting hatred by denying the existence of the Holocaust and teaching that Jews were very undesirable people. "Arguments ... centred on the distinction in the law regarding the right of free speech and expression and the protection of minorities from slanders and libels."[70] Keegstra maintained he had the right to express himself as guaranteed in *The Canadian Charter of Rights and Freedoms*[71].

After 14 years of trial, retrials, and sentencing,[72] the final verdict was a one-year suspended sentence (that is, no time to be served), one-year probation, and 200 hours of community service. In other words, nothing, although at one juncture all justices of the Supreme Court:

"agreed that the crime [expressing an untrue and unsavory opinion] violated freedom of expression. However, the majority concluded that the law was justified as **a reasonable limit on freedom of expression** because hate speech might lead to psychological harm, degradation, humiliation, and violence."[73]

---

[70] MERT, STEVE and JOHN WARD, *Keegstea The Trial. The Issues, and The Consequences*, Western Producer Prairie Books, 1985.

[71] *Charter of Rights and Freedoms*, Section 2 (b): freedom of thought, belief, opinion, and expression, including freedom of the press and other media of communication.

[72] The trials had enough global coverage to have a 1988 television movie made. It was named Evil in Clear River in which Keegstra was played by Randy Quaid, the brother of better-known actor Dennis Quaid. Randy fled to CANADA claiming "Hollywood Star-whackers" were out to get him. He was denied status in CANADA and arrested when he re-entered THE UNITED STATES.

[73] BOWAL, PETER, Professor of Law at University of Calgary, What Ever Happened to... Jim Keegstra, Law Now, July 1, 2012.

So, the question here is, is the title of this book a legitimate expression of free speech; or does it have the potential to "lead to psychological harm, degradation, humiliation, and violence?" Of course not, so get over it.

Mr Bean (aka Rowan Atkinson, famous English comedian and professional engineer) warned against "a new but intense desire to gag uncomfortable voices of dissent" that could result in punitive actions for "criticism, unfavourable comparison or merely stating an alternative point of view".[74] In short Mr Bean questions if it is a function of the State to protect individuals from insults or even just perceived offensive comments, regardless of how vague they might be. As examples, he cites the arrest of one who said "woof" to two Labrador dogs; an Oxford student arrested for saying to a mounted policeman "excuse me, do you realize your horse is gay"[75;] and, among other examples, members of an LGBTQ group arrested while protesting against a fundamentalist group calling for the "killing of gay people, apostates, Jews, and unchaste women".

Mr Bean summarized in addressing the English Parliament:

"The clear problem with the outlawing of insult is that too many things can be interpreted as such. Criticism is easily construed as insult.
Ridicule is easily construed as an insult.
Sarcasm, unfavourable comparison, merely stating an alternative point of view can be interpreted as insult."

If it is concluded that something is intolerably insulting, Mr Bean says the most effective action is to talk about it, not to invoke laws. A good example is protesters in the 1960s America calling peace officers pigs. The officers responded the next day by wearing small lapel pins in the shape of pink pigs, which took the air out of that balloon.

---

[74] Digital Journal, Free Speech in the UK: Rowan Atkinson and the right to insult people, October 29,012.

[75] Mr Bean does not elaborate on who was offended and why, the officer, the horse, or both.

Is the title of this book a literary technique where two opposites are positioned against each other for comparison and emphasis; or is it somewhat pejorative or vaguely offensive; or, is it worthy of a court case seeking damages or punitive action? To begin, it is Mike Mountain Horse saying it to me, many times over, and loudly laughing each time, leaving one to infer that to him, it did not matter. To him, he was dirty from working with coal fueled steam engines; he was old, something we all experience although not always admitting; and the word Indian was a non-Indian word more important to non-Indians than to Indians.[76]

The modern significance of the title *"The Dirty, Old Indian"* MY CANADIAN HERO, is that the slender substance of the racial slur is diminished when placed beside the colossal contribution the slurred Indian has made to CANADA; and it serves to remind us that there are virtuous and courageous Mike Mountain Horses, as there will be into the future.

Using the remarks of the fictional Mr Bean's thoughts about freedom of expression (or in other words, freedom of speech) may not excite academics or jurists, but in the world at large the comedian's thoughts can be more forceful, in the same way that an editorial cartoonist can convey and elicit more comment and empathy with a simple drawing than can a full-page written editorial.

Millions more people around the world have heard, seen, or read Mr Bean's advocacy for freedom of expression, and ingested and passionately embraced his concept of what at times can be a very subjective, arguable, and controversial matter. For academics and jurists, millions of people around the word understanding or just reading their concepts is something for which they can only dream. Obviously, the comedian's comments are more livable by the common person than those seldomly-read comments of the experts and authorities.

---

[76] Placing two different ideas side-by-side for purposes of developing comparisons and contrasts is a well-known literary technique known as juxtaposition. The desired result is informed and democratic discussion.

Mr Bean's UK problem is current in CANADA. There is a bill (C-413) before Parliament (October 2024) that would criminalize any statement as:

> *"condoning, denying, downplaying or justifying the Indian residential school system in CANADA through statements communicated other than in private conversation".*

This is the most asinine, the most poorly thought through proposal in the modern world of preciously protected free speech. It is so insulting and stupid I will not give publicity to the moron who proposed it by mentioning her name.[77] Now, if this is not enough to perturb that free speech denying lawmaker, try this:

> *"the only abuse I saw were Indians abusing Indians".*
>
> (My Aunt, a Royal Registered Nurse during World War II
> and who was in residential school for eight years)

Pursuant to this Bill, I wonder if this above statement is a capital offense or just time in jail.

---

[77] Member of Parliament Leah Gazan: *"residential school denialism"*

Dr Seuss - Racist

There wasn't a horse that couldn't be rode ...
There wasn't a cowboy that couldn't be throwed.

I thought of this when thinking about what was and what was not offensive. There is no limit to what can be labelled offensive; and there is no one who is immune to being offended. It is opinion.

If something is said to be offensive, or someone feels offended, what is to be done. Is there a need to do something? Some would differentiate between personal and social offending. For example, one's baby might be called ugly, very much offending the mother, but nothing needs to be done here. The mother can ignore the comment and go on loving the child. She need not nor does she have the right to clobber the offender.

During the "flower generation" in San Francisco, rioting young people taunted the police by loudly calling them pigs. Social offence warranting police clobbering? The next day police wore little pig pink pigs on their uniforms, leaving the protestors momentarily bewildered and unfocused not knowing what to do next. The policemen's personal feeling for the need to do something was replaced by a subtle and successful, considered response.

In the situation with the ugly baby and the pigs, individuals determined the response, not government. However, government often cannot resist the urge to get involved. An example of a government official feeling the need to get involved was the American Attorney General who on his first day entering his new office ordered the breast on a statue of a woman in the lobby covered. Of all the gin joints in all the towns in all the world, he walks into the Department of Justice and offends millions of art lovers. There is no doubt that millions of Americans would support his prudishness and puritanism, even preach it. So let them, but do not deny others the freedom to embrace the human spirit that is expressed in art. It is a good thing the Attorney General did not see the naked art with Bojangles (I understand it's okay to say penis and testicles if it's in parenthesis) hanging out on the street in Calgary.

The unfortunate aspect of the Attorney General's imposition of his personal point of view is that by virtue of the office he holds his attitude spreads through society more easily and widely than the grumbling mumbling guy mixing concrete at a construction site in Cincinnati.

As Mr Bean argues, more problems arise as government takes on the role of proclaiming what is offensive and what is not. Even if government does not proclaim, it influences, as the Attorney General did with his order to cover the statue; and like President Donald Trump did calling his supporters to Washington with the result that they assaulted and broke into the Capital Building on January 6, 2021. He pointed them down the street to the Building and then cowered with a Cheshire cat like look in the White House.

The public follows elected officials, either directly or indirectly like the mob's assault on the Capitol Building, or indirectly, like the self-imposed censorship of Dr Seuss. Books by Dr Seuss enjoyed decades of prominence in thousands of schools and libraries though out North America. The libraires in Calgary have 61 copies of *"And to Think I Saw It On Mulberry Street"*[78], a Dr Seuss book written just before the Second World War. However, the estate of Dr Seuss Enterprises, acting on the advice of a "modern panel of experts", decided in 2021 that it would no longer

11 Art with bojangles hanging out

---

[78] In March of 2021, all copies were checked out and there was a waiting list for them.

publish the book because the book portrayed "people in ways that are hurtful and wrong"[79].

Now, I always felt the characterization of people in Dr Seuss books was weird, but the parody inherent in them reinforced the point he was making. In *Mulberry Street* he is highlighting the usual gap between young and old, and how hard it is to find the words to help expand his father's imagination. In the end, the little boy resigns himself to the reality that he will have to have patience with his father until the father grows up.

A Chinese boy
Who eats with sticks.   A big Magician   A reindeer beast   No s
                             Doing tricks.   That needs a comb.   I'm o

(This is the page of about 21 pages in the book *And To Think That I Saw It On Mulberry Street* that will no longer be printed. The offending characterization is the Chinese boy in the lower left corner, which is no more offending than any of the other characterizations.[80] When I showed a young girl of color about the boy she exclaimed "are your kidding"!)

Mulberry is great children's literature, but it will be published no more. In this case, government did not make this so but the Suess Estate

---

[79] THE NEW YORK TIMES, *Do Liberals Care If Books Disappear?,* March 2, 2021.
[80] Dr. Seuss, And *To Think That I Saw It On Mulberry Street*, circa 1936.

bowed to what it accepted as the social moral attitude of the time. It was not a business decision which would have compared the cost of publishing to the revenue earned. It was someone's idea of what would or would not offend society. There is no objective measurement of what would be offensive, like the rate of return on the investment in publishing. But the Estate held its finger to the wind and concluded that the book was, in the words of an Indian Chief I know, "pissing upwind", which is what the title of this book is doing:

"The Dirty Old Indian" MY CANADIAN HERO

A tribute to World War I hero

Many readers and activists of various kinds will not get beyond the first phrase: "The Dirty Old Indian". It is offensive and racist they will scream and shout. They can not reach the second phrase that is actually emphasized by the first phrase.

The difference between the two phrases is enormous and it is the three second sound bite of the first phrase that will be cited most often. The second phrase —that Mike Mountain Horse is a hero — is greater than it would have been alone. It is social commentary of the highest order.

On the one hand some people are laughing at the "dirty, old Indian", but on the other hand they are able to laugh because of what he as a soldier did for them.

And Mike Mountain Horse was perceptive enough to know that!

Mary Mountain Horse - Second Class Citizen

Mary Adeline Mountain Horse (1891-1956) was disenfranchised when she left the reserve. Her Treaty Rights, or Indian status, was taken away because she was female.

"Marry out — stay out" is a common sentiment, if not a policy, on reserves. On the Mohawk Reserve south of Montreal it was written policy. The council evicted a number of residents because they were in an inter-racial relationship. The evictions were formal notices from the Reserve Council, but they were anonymously supported by a large number of Indians who, presumably, met the criteria for Band membership: that is members "must have four Mohawk great grandparents".[81]

Mike remained a status Indian until he died because he was male. He is buried at *St. Paul's Cemetery*[82] on the Blood Reserve[83], while Mary is buried in Lethbridge's *Mountain View Cemetery*.

Mary was of the Kainai Tribe (named Blood by non-Indians)[84], part of the Blackfoot Confederacy, which is made up of seven tribes. Her father, Wolf Moccasin (Potaina), was given the non-Indian name of Joe Healy after the American bootlegger of that name[85] who adopted him

---

[81] CBC, *Kanhnawake Mohawk Council will not appeal Superior Court decision overturning 'marry out, get out policy*, June 6, 2018.

[82] "Most [grave] sites are unmarked and overgrown with thistle and prairie grasses … The cemeteries on the Blood Reserve are located at Old Agency, an original settlement on the vast reserve; St. Catherine's along Highway 2 at Stand Off; St. Mary's School, in an abandoned area with knee-high grass in front of the old residential buildings that burned down; …. Levern, on the western edge of the reserve along Highway 505; and St. Paul's, about two km west of the old residential school on the southwest section of the reserve". [GARY ALLISON, Lethbridge Herald, *Blood Reserve Cemeteries,* September 21, 1997.]

[83] "One of the most celebrated 'old boys' [of St. Paul's Anglican Residential School] was Mike Mountain Horse who enlisted during World War I and was wounded twice during the Battle of Vimy Ridge. He was awarded the Distinguished Conduct Medal." (The Anglican Church of Canada, St. Paul's School — Blood Reserve, Cardston, AB, https://www.anglican.ca/tr/histories/st-pauls-cardston/)

[84] Named Blood because ochre was their most used colour.

[85] Joe Healy's stepfather John managed a trading post at Fort Benton, Montana, the furthest up-river navigable point on the Missouri River. Fort Benton was the starting point for the Whoop-Up Trail, a wagon trading route (largely whiskey north and furs south), to Fort Whoop-Up, just outside of Lethbridge, after which it branched to Fort McLeod and to Standoff, the current administration center for the Kanai reservation. [Wild West, Jerry Keenan, The Whoop-Up Trail, April 2015.]

after his mother, father, and sister were killed by Pend 'Oreielle Indians along the Moriah River in Montana. After attending school for eight years in Helena Montana, Wolf Moccasin returned to his home in the southwestern corner of *Alberta* where he is buried. One of his pall bearers was Mike Mountain Horse who was the partner to his daughter Mary. Mary's sister married James Gladstone, the future Senator.

Unlike Mike, of whom much is known, the most that is known of Mary is that she was Mike's partner of more than 26 years. After she died, Mike lived with my family for over a year. He would say to me that he "needed to get a new can opener".

12 Mike and Mary at Dempsey's wedding

Mike was not being disrespectful; it was a term of endearment, I think[86]. I listened to Mike and Mary always quietly talking over the years, never raising their voices. I wish I knew what they were talking about, but they always spoke Blackfoot, not English. However, judging by the rare inflections (us' tuchka'tama) In her voice and Mike's docile responses, there was no doubt who oversaw the household.

---

[86] I remember my mother saying that Mike wrote his book at the insistence of Mary. She would tell Mike that he had all these great stories and memories and if he didn't write them down, they would be gone. Mom insisted that Mary was the driving force behind Mike's writing.

Mike Mountain Horse was trying to alleviate his grief over Mary Mountain Horse's death when he jokingly said he would have to get a "new can opener"[87]. That comment today would certainly arouse feelings of sexual disrespect.

Mary Mountain Horse was the victim of institutionalized gender discrimination, both ancestral and government. The government discrimination was in the *Indian Act* which withdrew women's treaty rights if they married a non-Indian. Ancestral because she had to hide on the floor of a car's back seat to visit her sister on the Reserve.

There were two Mary's in Mike's life. To which, if either, Mike was married is not entirely clear. The first Mary appears on his military *Attestation Paper* wherein it is stated that his wife is just Mary Mountain Horse. Corroborating documents expand on this name as "Mary Agnes Mountain Horse"[88]. When Mike was shipped overseas for *World War* I, he signed over his monthly pay, referred to as a separation allowance, to his "wife Mary Mountain Horse"[89]. Her address at the time was shown only as "10 Street, McLeod" where she would have been living with Mike before he went overseas because he was employed as a scout at the Fort for the Northwest Mounted Police

---

[87] Mary, like all grandmothers, was a great cook, especially of Saskatoon pie, the berries for which I would pick with her in the coulees of the Old Man River.

[88] *Attestation Paper*, Canadian Over-Seas Expeditionary Force, Folio 25, No. 895041; and, *Militia and Defence*, Separation and Assigned Pay Branch, Overseas Contingents, 20705.

[89] "… under the rules for enlistment introduced by the Canadian government, married men required the written consent of their wives in order to enlist." (Ian Becket, The Great War, 2007)

The Mary Mountain Horse I knew (my grandmother) lived with Mike from the early 1930s until her death in in 1956. The name on her daughter's birth certificate[90] is Mary Adeline[91] Healy.

13 Mary Mountain Horse's headstone

"I believe Mary was at peace with Mike".[92] Her headstone is Mary Adeline Mountain Horse.

Record keeping in white society is a different concept than it is in Indian society. So while white society is meticulous in keeping written records, Indian society is not, other than oral history which over time can be tenuous at best Therefore, it is difficult to find records, especially from those days, of marriages or divorces on the Reserve. People just lived together. In this situation, it looks like Mary and Mike lived together for a time, and then apart, and eventually together again. In the meantime, official white record keepers would have noticed and revoked Mary's Indian status, something they did not or would not have done to Mike. Clearly, gender discrimination.

An attempt was made to eliminate this discrimination by amending the *Indian Act*. *The Indian Act* revoked women's rights if they married anyone without "status", which means white people[93]. "The *Act* no longer requires ... women who follow their husbands into or out of status, and it allows women to pass status on to their children just as men always have."[94]

---

[90] Alberta, Certificate of Birth, B145442, September 6, 1922.

[91] Mike's enlistment paper shows her middle name as Agnes. The spelling on her headstone in Mountain View Cemetery in Lethbridge is Adeline. In any case she has a headstone, which cannot be said for her more renowned husband.

[92] LAWRENCE, YVONNE, *Healy Family Dinner & Conference*, October 7, 2023

[93] In his book *My People the Bloods* Mike notes that there would be less trouble between Indians and non-Indians "if each were to stay in their own pasture".

[94] MCNAB, MIRIAM, edited by Anne-Marie Pedersen and Tabitha Marshall, *Indigenous Women's Issues in Canada*, January 30, 2015

This amendment had unintended consequences. Women who had been disenfranchised but who were now added to Band lists meant that Band resources and revenues had to be shared among more Indians; that is, because there were more with whom to share, each got a smaller piece of the pie, resulting in resentment from those already on the lists. The newly registered Indians became disparagingly known as *"Bill – 31ers"* after the Parliamentary name of the amendment.

In any case, given the dearth of documents and the monumental effort it would take to trace treaty money, the documents that are available would leave one to conclude that Mary <u>Adeline</u> Mountain Horse lost her treaty rights somewhere along the line — and thus became a second-class Indian, an institutionalized gender discrimination much more consequential than gender discrimination in white society. Nevertheless, she successfully raised five children all of whom were full participants in and contributors to Canadian society.

Mary Agnes Mountain Horse was born about 1889 on *Kainai #148, K 50 Little Ears Band* and at age 5 was enrolled in St. Paul's Residential School for 13 years[95]. She and Mike were probably schoolmates.

Before World War I when Mike was a scout for the Northwest Mounted Police he lived on the very southern outskirts of Fort Macleod. Now, one can only imagine why this was so far out of town and might conclude that it was a "wrong side of the tracks" part of town; and given the temper of the times, that the

14 Mike Mountain Horse's home before WWI

---

[95] Ibid, Lawrence, Yvonne.

residents so far out of town were Indians. Leave it for the *Fort Macleod Historical Society* to prove otherwise.

The house that Mary Adeline and Mike lived in during the *Second World War* was a big improvement from Mike's *First World War* house. It was in Lethbridge. There was a balcony in the front (the front had a picket fence and the back a five-foot no space boarded fence), and the house included a large kitchen with a black iron stove and a box of coal for fuel,

15 Mike Mountain Horse's home after WW II

which I as an unattended child managed to set ablaze. The living room was filled with a six-place heavy mahogany dining table and an adjoining bedroom. In the corner of the living room was a small fridge sized, hand cranked phonograph player with a stack of Wilf Carter and Gene Autry cowboy records.

In one way though, the *Second World War* house was the same as the *First World War* house. It was still on the wrong side of the tracks, even though Mike, based on his union sized railway paycheck plus Treaty and military[96] money, could certainly fit in the top half of Lethbridge's upper middle class on the "right side of the tracks". One can only imagine.

Mary Mountain Horse taught me how to braid leather strips. She did not say what the strips were for, but I have assumed they were used for horses, but given what I do not know about horses, I could not say for what or for what end of the horse.

She also showed me how to make a "sling arrow" and how to shoot it. I showed my younger brother and he got sufficiently skilled

---

[96] Although Mike probably did not get a military pension as Indian veterans were declared ineligible.

over time to hit a cardboard box with enough velocity that the arrow went right through it.

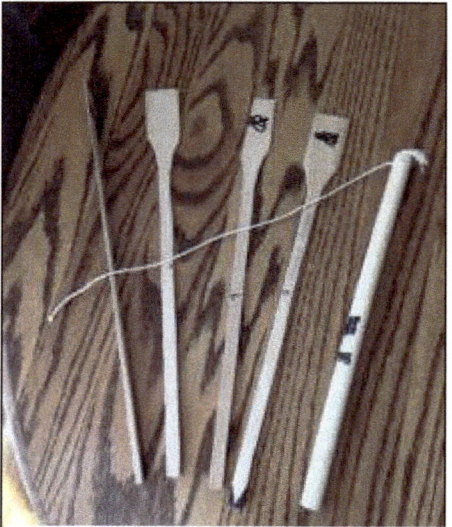

16 Sling arrow, don't try this at home

A generation later, I showed my young grandson how to make a sling arrow. On his first shot from the back steps of my house, he shot the arrow across the back yard and over the street past the front yard into the neighbor's flower garden. He was gleeful, turning to me he said, "if we sharpened the point of the arrow it would stick in the ground". Or into something else I realized and quickly turned his attention to something less dangerous. I wonder if the arrow is still there.

My brother, the one pictured with Mary Mountain Horse on page **Error! Bookmark not defined.**, made a sling arrow with his young granddaughter. He had more sense than I though. He painted the point on the tip of the arrow rather than sharpening it.

17 Mary Adeline and her dog Buster (and Mike)

Heritage – the modern reality

As a young boy I was in awe of Mike Mountain Horse's life. I thought about, but could not image the shock he went through, from a young man living a simple life on the prairies to the horror of the human slaughter in World War I. He told me stories, but that is all I thought they were. He did not embellish them, I do not think, nor dwell on the trauma. There was no post-traumatic stress that I could see.

He was ordinary. He was employed the duration of his working life. He was quiet, lived with my grandmother Mary[97] until she passed away. I never heard a hard word between them.

Neither ever drove a car nor flew in an airplane. I did not see them use a telephone; they did not have one in their home. Their lifespan ended with television and nuclear bombs.

I was always proud of my Indian heritage, when I was young, and would proudly tout it at any opportunity. Mike and Mary Mountain Horse were very special to me. They were the only role models I ever had. When ever Jimmy Gladstone was mentioned, I would say that's my cousin, wishing I looked as much Indian as he did. At a celebration of Jimmy's life organized by his sister in the Outrider Bar in Calgary I spoke and said pointedly to the room of almost all white cowboys, that Jimmy was my cousin, and I was proud of it. Two days later, another celebration of Jimmy's life was held in the Cardston arena. The arena was almost all Indian. I didn't speak.

I wanted to apologize because between that arena and our young days together, my heritage was publicly tarnished, and I did nothing to improve it. The modern image of Indians was not a good one. Living in a large city, many of the Indians I saw were derelicts – passed out on the

---

[97] Note: During the War, Mike assigned his pay to his wife Mary Mountain Horse (Government of Canada, Militia and Defense, Assigned Pay, Overseas Contingents, M. F. W. 11. Regimental Number 895041).

However, after the War, once Mary left the Reserve, she lost all her Treaty rights. Mike, being male, of course was allowed to keep his. It would be interesting to know if this blatant gender discrimination was Canadian Government or Tribal.

transit or yelling for everyone to get off the train because it was on Indian land. Or seeing them panhandling in the Mall, or one time just sitting down at my table and helping himself to my fries. The same type of thing happened to me at the Sarcee Indian Rodeo. I was standing in line at a concession, next to be served,[98] when an Indian wearing a big cowboy hat stepped in front of me and said, "this is my land".

I met this same Indian years later when he was a Councillor for his band. It was in the board room of a magnificent looking reserve administration structure that had a grand panoramic view of the foothills with snow covered mountains. Of course, he did not recognize me, but I had not forgotten him. I was asked to introduce myself and in doing so said that I was interested in politics. He was sitting near to me and I could hear him say under his breath "wait until he tries Indian politics"[99].

I was there proposing an overseas project, for which they had, in my opinion, some expertise to contribute. For years, they had been finding and removing unexploded ordinance from their land that been leased during the Second World War to the Canadian Department of Defense for artillery practice.

After the meeting, the band administrator approached and said, "walk with me." He knew me many years earlier from basketball. He did not know that I remembered him from basketball too, but also from his boasting that he could hit a gopher at thirty feet with a rock from either hand – simultaneously. We both laughed at the audacity of the claim. Years earlier, his all-Indian team had played in a basketball tournament and had won a great deal of respect for their effort the first night. The next morning, they were scheduled to play again, but only four players showed up, without shoes, which were not needed anyway because they were falling-down drunk. My team sat on the sidelines, not disappointed because these types of things were what some had come to expect of Indians. The band administrator was one of the players.

Walking with the administrator, he explained to me that the people in the room were different than I was, and I had to allow for that.

---

[98] When a five-year manager of a Vernon hotel with 100 employees was asked by a reporter why no Indians worked there. His reply: "Because none ever applied."

[99] Steve Runner, eight years a Band Councillor for Tsuut'ina, and also an Administrator and Executive Officer.

They were different, he went on to explain, because they had fiduciary rights – whatever he felt that meant, I got the message.

Anyway, based on a Canadian foreign aid program we got the project which was in PANAMA.

The first trip to PANAMA, I ended up paying the costs of one of the project members because he had spent, or lost, all of his per diem (about $1,000) in one of the local bordellos. The Second trip, the project members refused to leave their five-star hotel to train locals in bomb detection because, they explained to me, they did not want jobs, they just wanted dividends. Given another chance to share their expertise with an African country, the project leader declined, taking me into her confidence and saying "Black people aren't like us"[100].

Our country hosts were not impressed. You're welcome to come back anytime the Panamanian said in a telephone call to me, "but please don't bring those Indians with you".

This started me wondering, had I ever seen an Indian working in Calgary, despite the reserves contiguous to the city. In our project country of PANAMA, the local Indians could be seen working in all kinds of jobs, from sweeping the floors in Burger Kings to bank officials. And they were always smiling. It was obvious that they liked what they were doing. The U.S. military in the PANAMA Canal Zone always sought out Cuna Indians to hire because they were so efficient. Ever since my five-year experience in PANAMA, I have kept an eye for working Indians in Calgary, and I have seen only one.

I think of an Indian youth I saw in a small *Alberta* court room. He was a prisoner who was appealing a seven-year sentence for manslaughter. Driving drunk, he had crashed into a car coming home from church and had killed several of the young occupants of the car. The courtroom was not suitable for this hearing, because it was so small, the parents of the dead were seated not more than ten feet from the appealing prisoner.

The prisoner's lawyer was arguing that the young Indian's sentence should be reduced because "it was not his fault because he had just turned eighteen and, at that age, young Indians each received

---

[100] No racial group has a monopoly on discrimination, as this comment illustrates. It is multi-directional. In Bangkok, about to enter an elevator in the national oil company building, two Thai engineers occupying it told me to take the next one.

$40,000 from an oil royalty trust fund, and he had just bought a new truck and was celebrating [that is, he was drunk]". I could feel the resentment of the dead children's parents expanding and filling the room as if to explode. If I was one of the parents, nothing in the world would have stopped me.

My Mother would always vehemently say in a very adamant manner that she hated Indians, but she never said why and we were always afraid to ask why, which was so confusing because my grandparents were as Indian as an Indian could be. Decades later it took my daughter to clear this up for me. In discussing this book with her, she pointed out that it was not the Indians my Mother hated, it was the discrimination. As soon as she said that the light came on. She was right.

My sister confirmed this. She recalled our mother often complaining loudly about things people said about her. But she said our mother was not mad at those who said them but at the Indians who gave them cause to say them. She was referring to the publicly held image of drunken Indians along first avenue and in Galt gardens in Lethbridge.

After discussing this with my sister, I recalled children of the Displaced People (DPs) where we lived yelling at me too, but I was too young to understand, although from the tone of their voices I got the message. On the other hand, my mother recruited two older DP school children to protect me on my daily walks to and from school.[101]

My mother's final note, although it was indirect, about Indians was regarding the *Indian Act* and Treaty Rights. An amendment somewhere entitled Indians who had been disenfranchised to be reinstated, along with their descendants. Two of my mother's sisters, my aunts, applied and were reinstated, along with their children, my cousins. My mother did not apply, and according to my sister would not even talk about it. She said that her mother "wanted her kids to live without the Indian stigma and to get out of life what they put into it".

---

[101] Their names were Irene Bouscwa and Ilona Madachi. (Sorry girls, I have no idea how your names were spelled.)

I never knew, but now wish I did.

Apartheid — Canadian Indian reservations

Apartheid is a term that was used in SOUTH AFRICA to describe the segregation of whites, blacks, and coloured people. Apartheid has been used to describe Canada's Indian reserve system, but it is used most often by Indian politicians reproaching Canadian society in general:

> *"... in 1948 [South Africans] learned from the Indian Act of the government of Canada, that they [based] their apartheid system on the Indian Act in Canada"[102].*

"Some scholars say officials with Canada' Indian Affairs Department met with their counterparts in South Africa in the 1940s to discuss elements of the Indian Act that were eventually incorporated into apartheid, including a policy that required black South Africans to obtain a pass to leave their town or village."[103]

Of course, saying Canada's reserve system is much like South Africa's apartheid, which was widely condemned around the world, most vociferously by CANADA which led to the imposition of sanctions[104] on that country, is open to argument. Indian supporters will quickly grab the comparison and say yes, look how badly and unfairly they have been treated in CANADA, just like the blacks in South Africa. Canadians, who generally think of themselves as the most liberal and compassionate in the galaxy, quickly disagree.

But notwithstanding debates that meticulously point to large or small similarities or differences between apartheid and reserves, it remains that the two are very similar in their intent — racial segregation — and are equally obnoxious and loathsome. Apartheid and reserves have no place in Canada's society.

---

[102] GRAND CHIEF DOUG KELLY, President of Stolo Tribal Council in B.C., in *Chiefs reflect on apartheid and First Nations as Atleo visits Mandela memorial,* Gloria Galloway, Parliamentary Reporter, December 11, 2013.

[103] Gloria Galloway, Parliamentary Reporter, December 11, 2013.

[104] Sanctions were varied and their support was by degrees, but the world was self congratulatory when apartheid ended, although it took 25 years for that to happen (which indicates that it was factors other than sanctions that ended it).

Why do Canadians tolerate the existence of reserves of which there are over 2,267 Indian reserves[105].

The Indian Act is archaic, obsolete. Even the title "Indian" is colloquially offensive. The *Act* should be abolished.

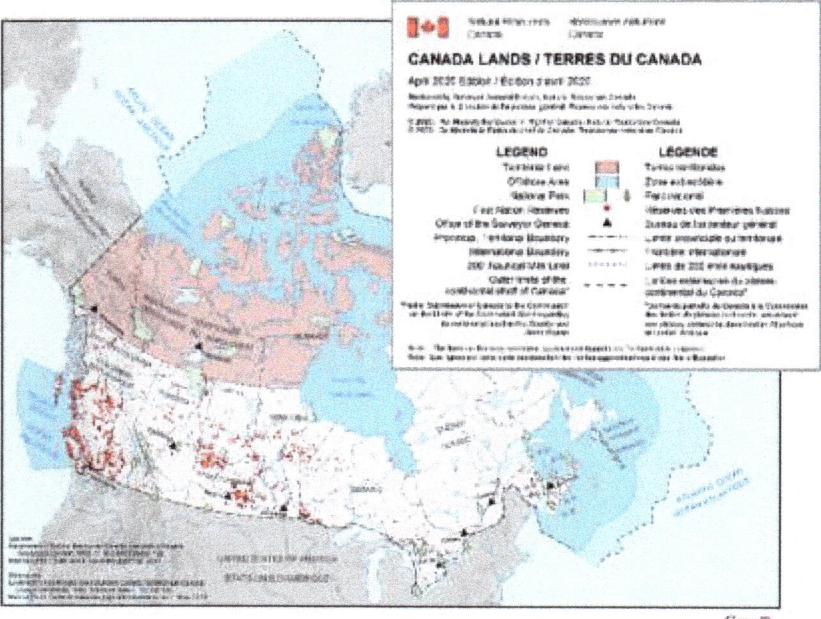

18 Location of reserves

However, Indians, or Indian leaders really, oppose ending the *Act*, even just amending it, and insist that their fiduciary rights be embedded in the Canadian *Charter of Rights and Freedoms*[106]. The reason there is opposition to ending the *Act* is that the Indian leaders fear it would

---

[105] GOVERNMENT OF CANADA, *Indigenous and Norther Affairs CANADA*, Reports. https://www.aadnc-aandc.gc.ca/eng/1100100034846/1100100034847

[106] *Charter of Rights Freedoms*, Section25. "The guarantee in this Charter of certain rights and freedoms shall not be construed so as to abrogate or derogate from any aboriginal, treaty or other rights or freedoms that pertain to the aboriginal peoples of Canada including a) any rights or freedoms that have been recognized by the Royal Proclamation of October 7, 1763; and, b) any rights or freedoms that now exist by way of land claim agreements or may be so acquired. Section 35. (1) The existing aboriginal and treaty rights of the aboriginal peoples of Canada are hereby recognized and affirmed. (2) In this Act, "aboriginal peoples of Canada" includes the Indian, Inuit and Métis peoples of Canada.".

result in the end to the reserve system. Ending the *Act* would lead to private land ownership by individual Indians, instead of collective ownership by the tribe. And individual ownership would see individual owners sell their individual pieces of land — and that sale would probably be to non-Indians. Thus, no more Indians.

And, no more Chiefs, with their large salaries and benefits. In other words, there is an incentive for Indians to maintain the status quo.

There is also an issue about "fiduciary" rights, which I do not understand. There are many legal definitions of fiduciary, but generally it means one party (in this case the Canadian Government) has an obligation to protect rights that must be exercised for the benefit of others (that is, Indians).

Riding on Calgary's public transit one day, a Drunken Indian at one end of the rail car started yelling that everyone had to get off his train. "This is my train; this is my land" he kept shouting. "I've got fiduciary rights" he managed to get out. Well, there is a lot to say about that, but my observation is that fiduciary rights to an Indian means give me more money. Just like in pipeline negotiations, Indian tribes will say no to development because they were not consulted. Of course, they were consulted. Pipeline companies know projects will get bogged down, justified or not, in court, if Indians or anyone say they are not consulted, so the companies make sure they are consulted. By saying they were not consulted, the Indians are simply saying give us more cash.

Most legislation starts with a bunch of "whereas" and then a "therefore". The reason for the "whereas" and "therefore" is to give the explanation or motivation for the act and the purpose of the act. *The*

Indian Act does not do that, it just gets right into it[107], more like regulations for administration of the reserves than legislation.

So, what is the purpose of *The Indian Act*? Why is there an Indian Act [108]? Does it follow, to be fair, that there should be an *Act* for every other kind of person in Canada — one for Blacks, another for Browns, Asians, Europeans, short people, tall people, people in airplanes. And, when talking about the *Act*, why is there a distinction for "First Nations"; what about second nations and third nations and fourth nations? Does anyone wonder about these questions or is it that we have heard "First Nations" for so long as an excuse, an all-purpose, hands turned up, shrug, that it just sails over our heads.

What were the legislators thinking when they passed the *Indian Act*, and did they think that it should go on forever? Most modern legislation has "sunset" provisions, or at least pauses for review, so that the provisions of the an act do not go on forever regardless of societal change and become irrelevant while continuing to live.

One of the first lines in *The Indian Act* defines bands as Indians "for whose use and benefit in common, lands, the legal title to which is invested in Her Majesty"[109]. Does this mean that reserves are owned by the crown, and not the Indians? Yes it does. The Act goes on to say, "designated lands means a tract of land or any interest therein the legal title to which remains vested in Her Majesty and in which the band for whose use and benefit it was set apart as a reserve ...". Furthermore, the *Act* defines reserve as "a tract of land, the legal title to which is vested in Her Majesty, that has been set apart by Her Majesty for the use and benefit of a band ...."

Mike Mountain Horse lived within Treaty 7, an 1877 agreement between the Canadian Government and the Siksika (100 kilometers east of Calgary), Kainai (north of Cardston), Pikani (north of the Kainai), Stoney-Nakoda (west of Cochrane), and Tsuu T'ina (on the south

---

[107] For Example, the First Nations Fiscal Management Act, S.C. 2005, c. 9, has nine "whereas" before it gets to a "now, therefore". [First Nations Fiscal Management Act 2005, c. 9 1; 2012, c. 19, s 658; and, the Indian Act R.S., c. 1-6, s. 1]

[108] The answer is that probably because reserves existed, and something was needed to administer them and to legitimize the surrounding White colonization.

[109] Ibid, S 2(1).

western edge of Calgary). It has about five "whereas" that helps make it clear[110] who is getting what and for how much. Treaty Seven says the Indian Tribes:

> *"do hereby cede, release, surrender, and yield up to the Government of Canada for Her Majesty the Queen and her [sic] successors for ever all their rights, titles, and privileges whatsoever to the lands included within the following limits ..... To have and to hold the same to Her Majesty the Queen and her [sic] successors forever[111].*

This is very clear, and it is clear what the Indians got in return:

> Land *"of sufficient area to allow one square mile for each family of five persons"[112]*

There are other concessions as well, some of consequence like education and livestock and tools for Indians' utilization of the land; there are others of less consequence, like individual cash payments, clothing, and guns.[113]

It is hard for someone today, Indian or non-Indian, to understand the reasoning or motivation used over one hundred years ago for the terms and conditions of a treaty, or contract, which is what the treaty really is, especially considering neither party spoke the other's language, despite the presence of an interpreter who gave his understanding of the treaty to the Indians, and then the Indians and non-Indians translated that interpretation into something else. In any case, the concessions the Indians received were in their eyes, at the time, of value, although they were undoubtedly of little consequence to the non-Indian side of the negotiations.

---

[110] A very informed lawyer I know with relevant expertise points out that when a lawyer uses the word clearly, you can be sure it is not.

[111] QUEEN'S PRINTER, *Treaty No. 7 between Her Majesty the Queen and the Blackfeet and Other Indian Tribes*, at the Blackfoot Crossing of Bow River and Fort Macleod, Ottawa, July 12, 1877

[112] Ibid.

[113] Ibid.

But now, using today's standards and comparing the economic advancement of adjacent non-Indian communities compared to Indian reservations, Indians want more, maintaining that they never gave up title to the land, ignoring they never had title. For example, a recent chief proclaimed:

"We never really did give up the land: Tsuut'ina chief urges public to see Treaty 7 document"[114]

The Chief goes on to interchangeably say they (Canadian government or Canadians. For him, I do not think there is a distinction between the two) haven't lived up to this part of the treaty yet or that part of the treaty"[115], but doesn't specify where Canada is delinquent. The Canadian Government (not including provincial governments) expenses more than $12 billion annually[116] on Indians; this despite the only annual requirement under treaties is that for education. On a per capita basis, this was $36,071 per Indian living on reserves in 2016, compared to federal program spending of just $7,316[117] per Canadian.

From my observation, Indians say that everything that is wrong on the reserve is the fault of the Canadian Government. Look what the Canadian Government has done to ud one said to me. Blame is never on those who live on the reserve.

Former Tsuut'ina Chief Lee Crowchild, quoted above, goes on to say "I wish that the residents of Calgary and surrounding areas actually come and read what the document [Treaty Seven] is ... because we wanted the treaty all along." It's obvious that Mr Crowchild should read the documents. I have read both *Treaty Seven* and *The Indian Act* and the Indians have gotten far more than the Canadian signatories could ever have imagined; or, that non-Indians intended.

The most important question about *The Indian Act* is "has it benefited the Indians; that is, has it enhanced or improved their standard of living". Today, is the standard of living on reserves comparable to that

---

[114] CBC NEWS, June 28, 2017. From Mr Lee Crowchild's comments, it seems he has never read the Treaty. Perhaps his lawyers have advised him to say he has not read the Treaty, giving his comments "plausible deniability".

[115] Ibid.

[116] Fraser Institute, *Small reserves, big salaries and new transparency*, in the National Post.

[117] Fraser Institute, Taxpayers are generous to first nations, in the Vancouver Province.

in non-Indian Canada? No emphatically, is the empirical answer. Firstly, from a theoretical point of view, isolating them on reserves prevents them from full participation in a broader community with a higher standard of living.

Secondly, from a practical point of view, using almost any measure, such as education, health care, per capita income, Indians lag non-Indians. Without any scientific evidence, other than common sense, the major cause of this disparity is *The Indian Act*. If, after more than a century this is where *The Indian Act* has gotten us, it is time to try something new — get rid of *The Indian Act*.

Why reserves?

Canadian reserves were created over a hundred years ago and there is little in the records to say why they were created. Circumstantial evidence suggests reserves were a *"colonial drive to 'civilize' Aboriginal peoples by introducing them to agriculture"*[118]. Another point of view was "The Act was created to enable the government to control these people [that is, the Indians], to stop their mobility and eventually to eliminate them as 'Indians' …. Reserve were created to control their mobility."[119]

Some reserves were created to facilitate non-Indian religious proselytization. And undoubtedly, they were probably created to build "fences" between Indians and those newcomers colonizing and developing the country so that one, the Indians, did not interfere or interrupt the settlers. Much of the reserve land was created by treaties (agreements) between the tribes and the Canadian government, others simply by decree of the Government, and some by grants from religious institutions, which of course had a self-serving motive.

---

[118] indigenousfoundations.arts.ubc.ca, What are Indian Reserves, https://indigenousfoundations.arts.ubc.ca/reserves/

[119] JEAN TRILLET, Maclean's, Why dismantling the Indian Act will be nearly impossible, Sept 24, 2017.

What if American Blacks were on reserves?

This is not a good comparison, because right away it would be pointed out that Blacks sold into White slavery suffered far more egregious deprivations than Indians on Canadian reserves, but even this would be argued, but mostly by Canadian Indians.

However, assume that American plantations where Blacks were slaves are somewhat like Indian reserves in that neither occupants were there by choice. After the American Civil War and Emancipation Blacks faced, and still do, outrageous institutionalized discrimination[120].

Despite less than full integration of American Blacks into White society, they have succeeded in becoming a part of that society. They dominate sports and sing the opening Stars and Stripes at big events (before stadiums full of Whites); there have been two Blacks on the U.S. Supreme Court[121] as well as a Black President, Barrack Obama and a colored Vice-President, Karmela Harris.

What if Blacks had been kept on plantations? Would Black Barrack Obama have become President of the United states? Twice?

What if Indians had not been put on reserves in CANADA. Would they be a more involved part of Canadian society?

Could an Indian have been Prime Minister of CANADA?

Why do Indians stay on reserves? They aren't fenced in; they don't need passes to travel off the reserves. If there are not jobs on the reserves, why not move to where there are jobs[122]? Millions of

---

[120] A personal memory I have of continuing discrimination in America is the story told me by a Canadian home from studying in Oklahoma. The student told how horrified she was when she saw that her 'Oklahoma classmates' favourite Saturday night pastime was to throw empty bottles at passing Blacks. This might appear isolated compared to "White only drinking fountains "and "negro lynching", but it illustrates the aggressive and enduring nature of the dilemma.

In 1921, a black community of Tulsa was "burned to the ground by a mob of white people aided and abetted by the National Guard ….. the death toll may have been as high as 300 ….. and an estimated 8,000 or more left homeless." [THE NEW YORK TIMES, *The 1921 Tulsa Massacre Many Want Forgotten*, June 21, 2020.]

[121] Clarence Thomas and the highly respected Thurgod Marshall.

[122] One young Indian man said to me they did not want jobs, they wanted dividends. This at a time when, Calgary contiguous to his reserve, was in the middle of an oil boom and crying for workers; and a major Canadian movie (Passchendaele) being produced on the reserve could not get workers either.

Canadians have moved to where there are jobs — Mike Mountain Horse did. If living conditions are not good on the reserve, why not move to where they are better?

How to end Canadian apartheid

Institutionalized Canadian apartheid is a Gordian Knot. A Gordian Knot is seen as a problem that requires a bold action to solve it. Over the years, attempts to solve the Indian problem have failed. Numerous initiatives have been rebuffed, by one side or the other, either Indians or Canadians. The status quo has festered.

A strikingly bold action is needed to solve the Canadian apartheid Gordian Knot. *The Indian Act* must be abolished to give Indians self-government and the ensuing capability to determine their own destiny. No amount of Government largesse or patronizing will motivate Indians to cultivate their own destiny. The Indian Act is a curse for both Indians and Canadians. It's time to end the *Act*.

Abolishing an act or agreement or treaty is not without ample precedent, either in CANADA or around the world. Parties to any of these were involved because it was in their interest to do be involved. When their interests change, they renegotiated or repudiated or abolished the agreements. GERMANY abolished its peace treaty with Russia only months after having signed it; THE UNITED STATES unilaterally initiated the renegotiation of NAFTA[123] after if determined CANADA and MEXICO were benefiting more than the US; CANADA abolished the *Crowsnest Pass Freight Rate Agreement* (which guaranteed western farmers a freight rate "in perpetuity") when eastern CANADA complained that its economy was being impaired by the agreement[124].

The Canadian government has the authority to walk away, to wash its hands of *The Act*. The *Act* belongs to the Canadian Government — it created it unilaterally — it can unilaterally repeal it. It is like the situation surrounding the *British North America Act (BNA)*. The BNA served as Canada's constitution for over 100 years. However, CANADA could not amend it to meet modern needs because it was a British Act

---

[123] North America Free Trade Agreement.

[124] Western farmers, who enjoyed the agreement, characterized the abolishment of the Act as "just another way for the east to screw the west", resulting in another outburst, although minor and confined, of western separatism.

of its Parliament. Therefore, the first step to be taken to amend it was to bring it, that is give it, to CANADA, which required another act of the British Parliament. The British parliament, because the BNA was its creation, abolished its ownership of the document. Canada now has the ability to determine its own destiny. Canada should do the same by repealing *The Indian Act*. A bold, and necessary action!

Reservations are a national disgrace. They blatantly target a specific ethnicity. The original social, economic, or political reasons for reserves has ended. It has been more than a hundred years since they were created. CANADA does not need another 100 years of disrespect.

CANADA loathed the segregation (apartheid) of Blacks in SOUTH AFRICA and led the international imposition of sanctions to end apartheid in that country. Whether or not the sanctions led to the end of apartheid is arguable since apartheid did not end for more than 25 years later. But apartheid did end, in large part because of how other nations disparaged the White Africans for imposing it.

CANADA always provided sanctuary for American Blacks escaping institutionalized slavery (the underground railroad, now an acclaimed television streaming series); and, now for evading social discrimination.

CANADA is justifiably proud of its human rights record and is seen by the world as a preeminent role model for nations. Reserves are blemish on this international image. Indian reserves are an unwanted contrast with Canada's role as the world's most important peacekeeper[125].

Reserves and modern Government programs for Indians are condescending, patronizing, and discriminating; and this has its origin and perpetuation in *The Indian Act*. It must be abolished, for the long-term benefit of the Indians, for the moral conscience of Canadians, and for the world stature of CANADA.

---

[125] Lester Pearson, at the time Canadian Secretary of State for External Affairs, won United Nations support for the creation of its first peace force during the "Suez Criss" in 1956. Ever since, Canada has been a major contributor of personnel and matérial for UN missions around the world. For his part, Mr Pearson was awarded the Nobel Peace Prize in 1957.

Ending the Indian Industry

The *"Indian Problem"* and the *"Indian Industry"*[126]. Most Canadians have never heard these terms, mainly because they never have, or have had to, deal with the Indians. That is because the Indians are over there, tucked away, out of sight, on reserves.

The *Indian Problem* generally refers to the apparent standard of living gap between Indians and non-Indians, measured by education, health, wealth, ad nauseam; and, Canada's never ending unsuccessful attempts to close the gap, mostly by throwing money at the problem, which despite the gap not changing in any significant way, continues to throw more money.

The most recent federal budget (April 2021) continues this folly. To "right historical wrongs" the budget has over $20 billion (including $2.5 Billion for distinctions based-early learning and childcare, whatever that is) "meant for short term-gaps".[127] That is equal to $60,748 per Indian living on a reserve.[128] This is in addition to the annual subsidy of $36,000 per reserve Indian. It is this kind of money shower that keeps Indians on reserves. Otherwise, they would do what millions of non-Indians have done – migrate to where the jobs are, like the Newfoundlanders who were a large portion of the *Alberta* oil sands work force.

The *Indian Industry* refers to the army of non-whites, consultants, lawyers, and others who walk arm in arm with Indians into government offices with grand schemes or claims that they maintain will solve the Indian Problem or that will remedy transgressions against Indian rights.

Canada and Canadians have no right to be in the Indian Industry. The Indian Industry and the Indian reserves are racist, a blemish on Canada's highly esteemed human rights' record in the world. Canada must get out of the Indian industry; reserves, if they continue to exist, must be Indian cooperatives, not Canadian mandated entities.

---

[126] "… the national native leadership, the many lawyers, consultants, advisers and academics, all government-funded, who would keep it going in perpetuity … "[Melvin H. Smith, O.C., The Fraser Institute, Aboriginal Land Claims in British Columbia: Serious Concerns About the Nisga'a Deal, 1998.

[127] Canadian Press, $18B Indigenous spending in Budget 2021 meant for short-term gaps", April 23, 2021.

[128] Appendix How many Indians are there, page 383

To get out of the Indian Industry, start by dealing with Indian "rights". Let us make it clear that there are no Indian rights — there are only Canadian Rights! Not Swedish rights, not Italian rights, not Ukrainian rights, just Canadian Rights that are the same for every Canadian. There are no different classes of Canadians.

If Indians do not accept this, then they can have the alternative that they have been demanding — self government[129]. Self government means having control of all the things on the reserve, much like, for example, Calgary, a Canadian community. But self government also means self supporting, something that seems to be outside the vocabulary or understanding of Indians; that is, they can pay for their own self government, and that means taxes, which they do not pay now. The situation now is that they do not pay taxes yet expect the benefits of a country; that is, they are taking more out of the Canadian pie than they put in.

The *Assembly of First Nations* goal of "entrenching" the right of self government in the Canadian Constitution is frivolous and absurd. There are broad and substantial benefits from acting together; that is why people band together to form countries. (CANADA is like a McDonald's hamburger franchise, page 141).

In touting sovereignty, the Assembly neglects to mention the other side of the coin:

self government → self supporting.

The only thing constant in life is change, and that includes agreements, treaties, and Acts[130].

This gets CANADA out of the "Indian Industry". We no longer will be responsible for what the world-condemns as apartheid. We will not

---

[129] Self government, like everything else Indian in this country, has been analysed and studied to death. For example, Parliament's Special Committee on Indian Self-Government (1983) for which the terms of reference were, among other things, "The status, development and responsibilities of band governments on Indian reserves, as well as the financial relationship between the Government of Canada and Indian bands".

[130] Canada just concluded the renegotiation of the North American Free Trade Agreement; America scrapped its nuclear pact with Iran; Canada scrapped in 1984 the Crowsnest Pass Agreement that guaranteed "in perpetuity" the freight rate for western grain (but not processed grain products, which distorted the economy because Western grain was thus processed in the east); etcetera.

have to apologize to THE UNITED NATIONS, where Canadian Indians have taken their case[131], that although Canadian apartheid is bad, it is not as bad as was African apartheid.

However, despite these apologies, CANADA should never have been, and should not continue to be, in the Indian industry or apartheid or reserves or whatever it might be labelled. It was wrong, and it is still wrong and should be phased out, if not immediately stopped. Whatever short-term pain this entails for both Indians and non-Indians, it will benefit all of us in the long term. The longer it takes to act to end Canadian apartheid, the problem will grow like a cancer to the detriment of future generations.

Instead of playing the worn-out racist card repeatedly to counter allegations that their plight is of their own making, show us differently. Instead of building casinos on the reserve, build training centres or technical schools or colleges or universities or medical clinics, things that are investments for the future, rather than dividends for immediate distribution and spending. Build on their strengths, whatever that might be, like their connection to the land, that they claim, which by implication non-Indians do not have,

---

Sharing rights means accepting reality

The only thing constant in life is change[132], and that applies especially to the way we relate and live together, which should be considered by those who cling "to the old way of doing things".

In the modern era, it is no longer a question of archaic Indian rights; it is a question of recognizing reality, and the reality in contemporary Canada is a quest for protection and preservation of equality, esteem of and respect for the individual. That means, from the non-Indian

---

[131] For example, "… we had a chief who went to The United Nations in New York on our behalf to talk about our land and our rights." [MacLean's, Few Canadians ever set foot on a First nations reserve, June 8, 2018.

[132] According to an ancient Greek philosopher which of course makes it true.

point of view, Canadian rights; it does not mean Canadian rights and Indian rights or Ukrainian rights or Chinese rights.

If the Indian position is that there are Indian rights and nothing else, as it seems to be[133], then there is an irreconcilable problem, and in the long term the majority of Canadian rights supporters is unquestionably going to dominate, thus losing the opportunity for us to use our differences to build something better.

The assertion of Indian rights seems to have its origin in the self-described label of "First Nations". "First" immediately raises the question of second and third and fourth etcetera; and it follows, what are the rights of each of these levels of people, and ultimately, which level is Canadian?

And clearly, if first nations have more rights than second nations, then second nations must have more rights than third nations etcetera, until we get to the point where F_n Nations have very few rights, or for all practicable purposes, none. Then what will we do, how can we tell who has what rights and who does not. Perhaps we could color-code rights and have each F_n Nation wear an arm band that is coloured according to the level of rights. Uh, wasn't this tried in Europe .....

Coloured arm bands could be a problem though for those diehard Canadians who think this might be problematic; that is, discriminatory. No problem. There could be a law, considered a typical Canadian compromise, mandating that coloured arm bands must be worn underneath shirt sleeves so they would not be noticeable.

Fabricating arm bands could be used by government to stimulate the economy. It could be stipulated that only certain economically underperforming regions of the country could make and sell them; and employment could be boosted by creating a national arm band inspection force that made sure people were wearing the proper coloured arm band.

Are coded arm bands any more ridiculous than having Indian rights and Canadian rights and their respective advocates arguing paramountcy? Not really, if you really think hard about it, which Canadians

---

[133] Indians who blockade railway lines justify their illegal actions by saying that they do not recognize Canadian law.

are prone to do if really pressed (for Canadians who do not think too hard, the word "really" is used three times in one sentence).

So, what to do. Keeping it simple, because the Gordian knot of Indian affairs is impossible to unravel, the first thing to do is for the Canadian government to eliminate *The Indian Act* which it has the right to do so because it gave itself the right to create it in the first place and thus has the right to abolish it.

Secondly, sovereignty must be recognized and respected, that is, enforced. There can not be Indian laws and Canadian laws. There must be one or the other. The choice is for Indians. If they say they do not recognize Canadian law, then they can retreat into geographic enclaves and have their own sovereignty with their own laws. However, that means they also have to develop the means to enforce those laws and build a society to support them. That means that Canada will no longer support them financially. They will have to pay their own way, without the benefits of being Canadian. And they will need passports to leave those geographic enclaves and enter Canadian territory.

Or, if they choose Canadian sovereignty, they have the same rights as all F_n *Nations* to form municipalities for local self-government.

Canadian living is sought by people from all parts of the world, a testimony to the benefits of being Canadian, yet Indians go before THE UNITED NATIONS and claim "genocide"[134]. The only genocide Indians living in Canada face is sefl-genocide from not adapting to the modern world. Continue the old ways and some day in the future young children will ask "what's an Indian".

Missing in all the demands for rights is the concept of responsibility. It is not unreasonable to expect, if not demand, that rights must be earned, and the way to earn them is to be responsible. Responsible by working each day, the very fundamental necessity of providing oneself food and shelter; and by working together providing enough and

---

[134] "Our conviction is that Canadian policy over more than 100 years can be defined aa a genocide of First Nations under the 1948 UN Genocide Convention. ... [Canada] ... engaged in a deliberate policy of genocide both cultural and physical." The authors go on to say that until Canada "engages in a National conversation" about this genocide, "we will never heal". Given the history of Indian claims, one could be excused for seeing healing as a code word for money and asking how much? (GLOBE AND MAIL, *What Canada committed against First Nations was genocide. The UN should recognize it*; Opinion, by Phil Fontaine and Bernie Farber, May 11, 2018.)

better food and shelter so that everyone benefits. Blockading railway lines is the antithesis of working together to provide food and shelter — it denies people food and shelter; it is irresponsible, and no one benefits.

Rights must be earned, and it would be difficult for Indians to demonstrate that they have earned the rights they demand from Canadians, and that Canadians have generously shared with them.

You can't legislate stupid

Legislating against racial discrimination is like legislating against stupid. It might reduce some of it, but it is not going to eliminate it. The best that can be hoped for is that it will be eliminated from the laws and institutions – that is, systemic discrimination.

Other than that, the solution, that is as good as any to end racial discrimination, is:

> *"a voluntary, free spirited, open-ended program of procreative racial deconstruction. Everybody just gotta keep fuckin' everybody til they're all the same color."*[135]

"Idle no more" - getting jobs

In 2012 another Indian protest was launched titled "Idle No More". It was welcomed, because without an explanation, it seemed to mean that Indians were advocating getting jobs, thus addressing one of their main complaints, unemployment.

Unfortunately, a closer look showed that Idle No More was a "revolution to honour Indigenous sovereignty And to protect the land & water"[136].

---

[135] Warren Beatty's character in the movie Bulworth, 1998, which he wrote, directed, and starred and for which he was Oscar nominated. The f-word is used 111 times in the movie.

[136] IdleNoMore, Home Page, idlenomore.ca.

Having a sovereign country within a sovereign country is contra-dictory. A country is either sovereign or it is not. Dual sovereignty does not work. It is like having two different systems of laws, so that for one person driving down the street they must be on the right-hand side; and, for another person they can drive on the left side of the street. How is that going to work out for you?

But sovereignty means much more than that and there are innu-merable formal, credible, and authoritative, philosophical, and legal dis-cussions about what it does mean. Even the Indians, while unanimously declaring it as their common goal, in practice leave many shaking their heads. Part of the problem in answering the question *"Sovereignty: Do first Nations Need it?"* "is the misunderstanding Indigenous people have about what Sovereignty really is" [137].

The debate about sovereignty will go on for as long as we let it. However, we have lived as one nation for so long, and not as F_n *Nations,* that nothing is going to change that, except civil war, and nobody will win that.

The issue of Indian's environmental responsibility causes much public ire. In the first place, it is bandied about with *a holier than thou attitude,* which is not a good starting point for discussion. Furthermore, the implication that Indians have more environmental expertise, or more spiritual appreciation when it comes to looking after the land, challenges patience.

Covid-19 — Indian immunity

In February 2020, various Indian groups and mostly environmen-talists blockaded rail lines across CANADA. Given the major arterial role of the world's largest railways, the economic damage from interrupted national and international shipments for all Canadians was in the hun-dreds of millions of dollars.

---

[137] Stephen Ford, Sovereignty: Do First nations Need it?, December 23, 2013. Mr Ford is a Mohawk Lawyer and Legal Academic.

In March 2020, the federal Government announced "it is spending $305 million to help Indigenous communities deal with the COVID-19 pandemic"[138].

In April 2020, just weeks later, *The Assembly of First Nations* said that aid to combat COVID-19 "is not proportional to the populations in their communities" compared to non-Indigenous communities. The Assembly "is calling on Ottawa to immediately make available 10 per cent of the future [national] funding … to Indigenous COVID-19 response"[139].

In April 2020, the Federal Government announced $396.8 million in funding for Inuit, First Nations, and Metis owned business. "The Government of CANADA is taking action to make sure that Indigenous business owners have access to the support they need to get through this [COVID-19] crisis."[140] The Prime Minister said the aid would help 6,000 Indigenous owned businesses, which equals over $50,000 dollars per business!

The total of these two handouts is over seven hundred million dollars, or, at $1 a face mask, about 418 face masks per Indian.

With such an obscenely unappreciated and one way flow of money it is easy to understand the frustration of the Manitoba truck driver who drove his rig through an Indian barrier and the *Alberta* roughnecks who dismantled and hauled away another.

The Assemblies claim that the aid Indians are getting is not proportional to their percentage of Canada's total population is an interesting statement and raises the question of just what the proportion is.

---

[138] CBC, First Nations welcome $305 million COVID-19 fund, March 18, 2020, https://www.cbc.ca/news/indigenous/first-nations-covid-funds-coronavirus-1.5502062

[139] The Globe and Mail, More coronavirus aid, PPE needed for First nations and Metis, leaders say, April 8, 2020. https://www.theglobeandmail.com/canada/article-more-coronavirus-aid-ppe-needed-for-first-nations-and-metis-leaders/

Furthermore, they want the funding without strings attached. They do not want the government telling them how to spend their money; that is, the money the Indians got from Canadians. Once Canadian money reaches the reserve, there is little accountability.

[140] Nunavut News, *Trudeau announces $306.8 million for Indigenous businesses*, April 18, 2020. https://nnsl.com/nunavut-news/trudeau-announces-306-8-million-for-indigenous-businesses/

Statistics Canada's most recent census (2016) show that there are 332,675 reservation Indians out of a total Canadian population of 35,151,728, which is about 0.9% [141]. Yet the Assembly thinks 10% of national COVID-19 funding for Indians would be more equitable. Off reserve Indians are not included in this calculation as they receive the same aid as all other Canadians.

Proportionality of out-put, that is in this case, national anti-virus funding, raises the question of input. If output is to be proportional, then so should input. CANADA measures input and output and expresses the result as Gross Domestic Product (GDP), which is the monetary sum of all goods and services produced in a year, including government. Provinces do likewise, the measurement being Gross Provincial Product (GPP). It would be interesting to calculate what percentage of GDP or GPP that is accounted for by Indians and compare that to see if it matches the 10% to which the Assembly feels it is entitled. Indeed, it would be interesting to calculate the Gross Reserve Product, minus the portion received from Canadian Governments. It would be very pleasing if this could be proven a positive number.

In any case one could wonder what the money from CANADA would be used for since it seems that money Indians receive is, in their opinion, without strings attached; that is, once the Indians receive it, it is nobody's business how they spend it.

---

[141] Statistics Canada, Census Profile, 2016 Census. https://www12.statcan.gc.ca/census-recensement/2016/dp-pd/prof/de-tails/page.cfm?Lang=E&Geo1=PR&Code1=01&Geo2=PR&Code2=01&SearchText=Canada&SearchType=Begins&SearchPR=01&B1=Aboriginal%20peoples&TABID=1&type=0

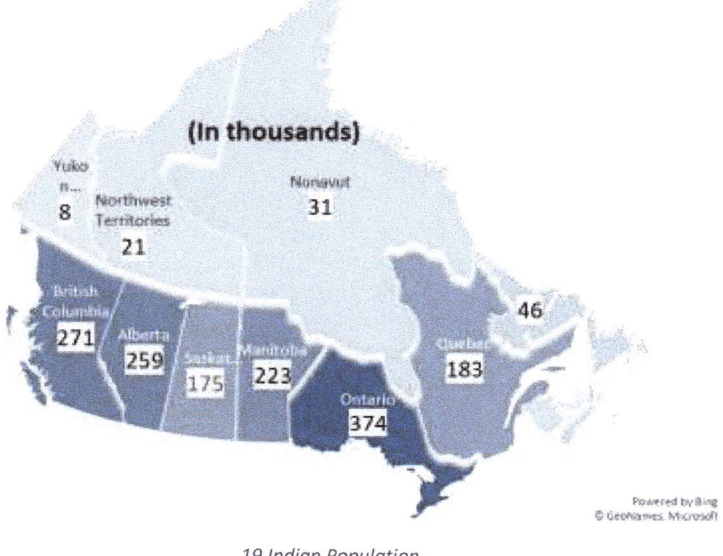

1,673,785 Indians in CANADA

(In thousands)

19 Indian Population
(Statistics Canada)

The Covid-19 pandemic affects all people, not just one national or ethnic or social or age group; it attacks any human with which it comes into contact, and spreads rapidly among people who are clustered, and the more humans congregate together, like in nursing homes or schools or theatres or restaurants or Sun Dances, the easier it is for one human to contaminate another. And what unique expertise do the Indians have to effectively decide how to use the millions of dollars to fight the virus.

So, to fight the spread of the virus, medical experts advise, and governments around the world have adopted the advice, social (physical) distancing — keep two meters away from others. However, "the Federation of Sovereign Indigenous Nations in Saskatchewan said, "provincial public health orders do not supersede First Nations laws" and immediately held a Sun-Dance to prove it. Canada's Indigenous Services minister said, regarding large Indian gatherings, that "they will be allowed to continue despite restrictions put in place due to COVID-19. Even in the face of a historic pandemic, CANADA must not and will not prohibit these important practices."[142]

What in the world was the Minister thinking? Is he thinking he is making the grand gesture, not acting like settlers in the old days? Is not their life, and that of their neighbors and food suppliers, more important than Indian ceremonies? Come on man, there are situations when the common good must take precedent over personal liberties, even Indian liberties, and a pandemic is just such a situation. If our society is to work, and Indians are part of that society whether they like it or not, we must all drive on the same side of the road. If not, get off the road and suffer the consequences, and relieve others from paying and caring for your stupidity.

Consider the thousands of churches in CANADA that are closed, helping to stop the spread of the virus. Their ceremonies and religions are just as good and important as those of Indians. The government ignoring Indian transgressions of the law is patronizing and denying Indians the motivation to grow from wards of the state.

Furthermore, the Federal Government is treating Indians differently when a common initiative is needed to fight a common malaise, the Covid-19 Virus. The Government "will spend another $650 million to help Indigenous communities cope with the COVID-19 pandemic ….

---

[142] msn | news, Minister says Indigenous ceremonies to continue despite COVID-19, May 14, 2020, https://www.msn.com/en-ca/news/politics/dark-stain-minister-says-indigenous-ceremonies-to-continue-despite-covid-19/ar-BB145zVp

STUPIDITY! The result of this absurd and irresponsible attitude is "Sask. Indigenous communities have reached 'intense' phase of COVID fight, doctor says: People from First Nations at highest risk of being hospitalized or dying from virus, research indicates", CBC News, Dec 1 2020.

And the Federation of Sovereign Indigenous Nations then said that "COVID vaccine distribution must prioritize Indigenous communities ….. [because] access to the vaccine is a matter of treaty rights", CBC News, Dec 4 2020.

Summarizing this farce, first the Indians say federal health guidelines for social gathering does not apply to Indians, so they gather; second, consequently Indian communities are the most affected by the covid virus; finally, Indians should get the virus vaccine first. What?

This money is in addition to $305 million previously promised to First Nations reserves"[143]. Indigenous leaders "from across Canada" said that initial funding "would not be enough"[144]; and they will decide how the money will be spent.

This is $2,870 per reserve Indian. I'll bet a private contractor could inoculate every Indian for $100 each, saving the federal government over $900 million dollars. What is a federal taxpayer to conclude?

If for only transparency purposes, the question of why Indian communities are being treated differently must be answered. Is it not a case of racial discrimination when they are treated differently like this? This money has nothing to do with treaty obligations. And cannot surrounding small communities wonder why they are not being treated the same as Indigenous communities.

And where did the Indigenous communities get the medical expertise to say that initial largess from the federal government was not enough; and, that their medical expertise was sufficiently credible to convince the government to triple the money given the Indigenous communities.

While we are at it, how about age discrimination and how seniors are warehoused in Senior Citizens' Homes and Health Care Facilities. Being warehoused so close together it was easy for the virus to be spread and more seniors died. As the virus has mutated though, the incident of virus deaths has increased in younger age cohorts. But the idea has been floated in less informed blogs, Seniors are old anyway, so let them die. Not a unique nor immediately discarded idea as indicated in the movie *Logan's Run*[145] where Seniors are killed at the age of 30 years.

---

[143] APTN NATIONAL NEWS, *Additional $650M in COVID-19 aid bound for indigenous communities*, May 29, 2020.

[144] Canadian Press, Another $650M in COVID-19 for Indigenous communities, May 28, 2020.

[145] Michael Anderson, Director, Logan's Run, 1976.

In Mike's words

"Civilization — Bad and Good"

The quotes below are from Mike Mountain Horse's book. They are the voice of a witness to *Alberta*'s early history, now contributions to a modern social debate.

The first line in this essay, "Civilization — Bad and Good" — reveals Mike's understanding of interpersonal relationships. He does not, in criticizing, cite the person, but instead directs his comments at the person's policies or actions. It is the person's "civilization" that he faults, not the non-Indian. So often, in political debate, or in what is more like political defense, a critic will attack the person, as opposed to the person's arguments or ideas. This limp intellectual reaction is obvious every day in parliament and most blatantly today in American politics, as especially employed by Donald Trump, the former president of THE UNITED STATES.

The richness of Mike Mountain Horse's intellectual range is the compatibility between his present and his ancestry, which might be seen as fatalistic acceptance but which he combines for opportunity for his Peoples' future:

> *"I sometimes wonder how long it will be before your so called civilization extinguishes my people from the face of the earth."* [146]

Mike's reference to the non-Indians' "so-called civilization" is a simple, impossible to misunderstand, call-out, challenging those who disparage the Indians' culture. He is saying *what makes you think that your way of life is better than ours?*[147] He later answers this question for

---

[146] Mike Mountain Horse, My People the Bloods, Glenbow Museum, 1989.

The manuscript for this book was probably a collection of Mike's essays written before and during the Second World War. Some of the flowery or more eloquent language, I believe, represents the efforts of the book's non-Indian editor, an acknowledged Alberta aboriginal historian, who is well know as a champion of Indian culture.

[147] In a discussion with a young honours sociologist at Mount Royal University on her way to graduate school, she said to me essentially the same thing by asserting, not asking, "what makes you think [the Indians] want to be like us". My conceit was laid bare.

you by saying that non-Indian society should "stay in your own pasture", and we will stay in ours; but later, reading between the lines, it seems that he sadly knows this will not happen, as he echoes the wise admonishments of Chief Sandford Big Plume (page 62) and Charles Barkley (page 64), that is — deal with it and move on.

Mike's acceptance of the future starts with concern that his culture will be overwhelmed, run over by a non-Indian tsunami. He does not dwell on this but quickly settles to the obvious fact that they are outnumbered, and that is not going to change. But he does not fatalistically resign himself to this; instead, he resourcefully uses social jujutsu[148], the martial art of using another's energy and momentum to enhance one's own, to successfully complement the old with the new.

In spite of this, it is hard not to conclude that there is a sadness underlying Mike's book, that although he accepts change, he does not agree with it, hanging, perhaps clinging, to the old ways of doing things and the harmony he believes Indians have with nature. He gives credit to the "nobly exemplified" aspects of missionaries and the Police, but at the same time laments the collateral detritus:

"I am not, of course speaking of those aspects of civilization so nobly exemplified by the missionaries and the North West Mounted Police, but rather the chicanery, drunkenness, greed and deception, which made their appearances in conjunction with the finer phases[149] of the white man's code, and which, as usual with evil things, found so many willing pupils among my people.

---

[148] The term social jujutsu was described to me by Sam Detomasi, a Calgary high school student. Social jujutsu refers to manipulating a social groups' strengths against itself rather than confronting it with ones' own strengths, which is the essence of the Japanese military art of jujutsu.

In some ways it is like "cultural appropriation", but with an ulterior motive. For example, stores will include a Pride logo within its own during Pride Week; or, include the Black Lives Matter (BLM) message during Black America's quest for justice in 2020, but in either case there is not much to show that the stores really believe in either cause – they just see the commercial potential to increase sales (the ulterior motive).

[149] I think he is talking about components, as opposed to time periods.

"Where are the tall handsome healthy bronzed Aborigines of yesterday?[150] Most of them are in the Big Sands[151], the Indian settlement of the Hereafter where all are welcome, good or bad; their earthly sins are forgiven, and equal love is extended to all whose time on earth has expired. Surely a generous heaven!"

Mike laments the inevitable demise of the Indians:

"Where are the numberless thousands of Indians who once roamed the plains, valleys and mountains of this continent? Their hordes are now represented by a small and **ever diminishing number of Indians**.

"The bad influence of the white race has affected the Indian both directly and indirectly. The worst of civilization as introduced by the East[152], could but teach the Indian to swear, steal, drink and commit the many other crimes and atrocities which necessitate the Criminal Code of the white man. But indirectly, much disease and suffering, previously unknown, arrived with the "pale face"[153].

"Let us review the habits of the aborigine insofar as they affected his health. First, consider the Golden Rule of health preservation as taught in schools and prescribed by the family physician. Get plenty of fresh air. Sleep with the window open. Play outside. Walk, etc. The Indian lived the advice as to an outdoor existence. His home was a teepee with a large opening at the top for ventilation, an aperture which could not be closed. Sanitation in the nomadic days was no problem. At the least sign of accumulating filth of any kind, the dweller had merely to walk to take down his dwelling and move to a location which had been cleansed by nature for countless years. His food consisted of Buffalo meat, roots and wild berries. His susceptibility to colds and other ailments of the white men were unknown.

---

[150] As illustrated, perhaps, by the cover of his book (page 26).

[151] He often referred to the Happy Hunting Grounds, but I never hear him say the Big Sands. In either case, this is the closest I heard him talk about what happens after death, kind of a hint at religion?

[152] That is, everything beyond the Bloods' eastern horizon, and not just a reference to eastern Canada.

[153] Paleface is not a word that Mike would normally use except in a derisive sense. In using it, he is intentionally mocking the non-Indian reader.

"A party of Warriors enroute during very cold weather would often encounter a river frozen over, but with the ice not sufficiently strong to bear the weight of one man. One of the hardiest would be selected to cross the river first. This man would carry his clothing above his head, swim[154] the icy river, and with his flint build a fire on the far bank. On his signal the whole party would swim across, dry their clothing, warm their bodies around the fire, and then proceed on their journey probably through considerable snow. But none of them ever became the victim of pneumonia - not even the sniffle of a cold in the head would be discernible as a result of an experience which would probably kill at least half the party of a similar number of the red men today[155].

"It is therefore apparent that the early Indian's open air [sic] life, his staple foods, and his constant exercise, built up for him a constitution able to withstand any strain and hardship imposed on it during the time of a natural lifespan. By accident, old age, death in battle or clan feud, the early Indian made his trip to the Big Sands, but seldom through sickness which ravage the tribes today and which were introduced by contact with the white man.

"The diminishing ruggedness of the present day 'educated' or 'civilized' Indian Is due to his lack of knowledge in adapting to the too sudden change of habitation, food, and style of living introduced by the white man. It is to this class of Indian that I belong.

"When the Federal administration which looks after the needs of the Indians first negotiated the famous Treaty of 1877[156], one of the stipulations was the Bloods and other tribes would live on reserves under supervision of officials appointed by the government. They went on these reserves and their early homes were built by them under the supervision of officials, who apparently had not considered the matter of reconciling the new with the old.

"These homes generally were rude log shacks containing one or more windows that could not be opened, and no ventilation other than

---

[154] I am not sure how one swims while carrying a bundle over one's head.

[155] C'mon Mike. If this were a believable story, next winter the good citizens of Calgary would, as a preventative measure, be cutting through the ice on the Bow River and swimming to the other side where the Mayor would be tending a warm fire.

[156] This is Treaty 7, September 22, 1877 between the Canadian Crown and the Indians of southern Alberta, which included the Siksika, Kainai (Blood), Piikani, Stoney-Nakoda, and Tsuut'ina.

the door. Tents were substituted in many cases, and these also had but one means of ventilation - the door flap. The teepee dweller was used to a perpetual movement a fresh air from the doorway upward through the top opening. In the log shacks, the circulation of which was completely stopped, and in the tents it was diminished.

"Needless to say, the war party set forth no more; hunting was greatly decreased, the **outdoor life diminished accordingly**, and the Indians lived their fresh air existence less and less. **This I believe to be one of the chief reasons why the Indian became so extremely susceptible to tuberculosis**, and why that terrible disease became so prevalent among my people.

"The old hardy diet of the Indians was perforce cast aside and food which they had previously never eaten was given or sold to them. Decaying teeth became known to the Indians for the first time, with all the resulting elements. I have met Indians barely past middle age, with all their teeth gone — a 'civilized' and unpleasant experience unknown prior to the change of diet.

"The adaptation of the reserve Indian to his settled life, to the understanding of the sanitation that life demanded, to the ventilation of his new home, to the proper balance of ingredients in a new diet, was all too slow to meet the rapid changes which were forced upon him. The loss of a free and roaming life cost me and my people a very high price.

"The last and most deplorable cause of the diminution of the Indian population is their fusion with the white race. To quote the words of an Indian: 'let the two races keep within the bounds of their own pastures!' My people are becoming extinguished rapidly enough without an unprofitable and miserable fusion with another race. The very thought is abhorrent to the right-thinking man of either race, for who as yet has discovered a truly happy union between white and red? The better white men do not marry Indian girls[157], and our higher class of

---

[157] The reason why "better" White men do not marry Indian girls is not given and it is left for the reader to draw inferences, like with the movie Earth Girls Are Easy. It does, however, imply discrimination, that White men think they are too good to marry an Indian.

female youth, through instruction in racial hygiene, have no desire to intermarry.[158]

"On the other hand, there's no doubt that the Northwest Mounted Police have been considered by the Indians to be their greatest allies and protectors. A comparatively handful of brave men, this organization gained control of the entire northwest, cleared it of its worst characters, and made life there safer for all. Law and order were brought out of chaos only because the men who comprised the force were of sterling character, men who held their honor higher than the briber's gold and were willing to face quick death on the plains, or the slower finish on the trail in the frozen North, in the upholding of a traditional principle.

"Perhaps the first and hardest task of the Mounties was fighting the whiskey traders and preventing these men from providing the Indians with 'firewater', which always resulted in brawls and killings[159].

"A close second in the difficulty was the abolishment of tribal wars, which meant the end of the warrior, the highest calling in the eyes of the Indian male. Also, the Indians had to be discouraged in their business (for business it verily was) of stealing horses from ranchers and hereditary enemy tribes across the American line. To run a herd of stolen horses across the border in early days was considered by the Bloods as not only a profitable occupation, but a feat of gallantry and daring as well. For this reason, it took much time and patience to persuade the Blackfoot Confederacy to desist from the practice and to settle down to slower and much less honorable — in the Indians' opinion — business of horse-raising and agriculture.

---

[158] This is interesting. It is difficult to understand what it means, but difficult not to conclude using today's standards that it is extremely racist. During the first half of the last century, it referred to keeping a race homogenous by preventing inter-racial sexual intercourse. It was taken to an extreme by Nazi Germany. But given the meagre education Mike had, I think he was just saying that we (the Indians) do not like you (non-Indians) any more than you like us, so let's stay "in our own pastures".

However, just asking, what if a non-Indian were to say this today. Would the non-Indian be a racist and given sanctions? (please see "vaguely offensive", page 38)

[159] There is an irony here as Mary Mountain Horse's grandfather was adopted at Sun River, Montana by a Fort Whoop-Up whiskey trader named John Healy (page 361). Healy was later at Fort Benton, the southern terminal of The Whoop-up Trail on the Missouri River, where he was the Sheriff.

"Colonel James F McLeod, beloved officer commanding the Northwest Mounted Police, never broke his word to the Indians. He was an aggressive and bold leader who achieved results that went a long way toward making Canada the most law-abiding country of its size in the world. He was afraid of no one, and perhaps this was the secret of his success with the Indians, though he did not rule them entirely through fear. **The Indians did not understand the white man's laws, did not want them, nor in many cases agree with them**, but there was one quality which they did understand and appreciate to its fullest extent, and that was courage.

"But even courage alone could not win the case for the Mounties. What really made the Red Man adopt principles and laws foreign to them was that these laws were administered with such bravery, fairness and honour on the part of the administration and administrators that respect of the Indians was completely won. These were qualities which Indians loved, admired and from their viewpoint, had always practiced.

"Shortly after the police and missionaries arrived, the Indians settled on reserves allotted to them by the Treaty, and it was then that the missionaries began to carry on their onerous tasks. Very difficult it was for them, for first they had to learn the Indian language. Only the white reader who has struggled his way through an Indian dialect realize the difficulty of this. Secondly, they had to combat the various traditional practices prevalent among my people at the time. And lastly, they had to inculcate the principles of Christianity into the minds of the Indians.

"Three stupendous tasks! The tedious learning of a language from persons who did not understand the questions asked of them; the overcoming of resentment in order to change old and unsanitary customs; the teaching of a religion revolving entirely on the belief in one God, to prospective converts who already were supplied with more deities than they knew how to propitiate! However, the teaching of the missionaries was of a practical nature. They quickly perceived that they had to improve the living conditions of the Indians before they could hope to accomplish anything toward raising their moral and spiritual status, and it is chiefly due to this practical outlook that their teachings were eventually accepted.

"With the idea of setting the Indians firmly on their own feet industrially, farming instructors and agents were sent to the reserve by the government to teach them agriculture. Day schools were established where the Indian children were taught. Boys' homes and hospitals were erected on the various reserves.

"The missionaries worked hard for the welfare of the Indians on all the reserves, and great moral changes have been wrought. A new era dawned, the old life quickly passing away, and the Indians began eagerly to look forward to still further advances through the aid of those who were so nobly striving to help them. Today green fields of grain may be seen stretching for miles across the Indian reserves.[160]

"In the early 1890s, the Bloods had only begun to adjust to the new mode of life brought to them by a foreign race. The clothing worn by men consisted of a shirt, a pair of leggings worn with a breechcloth, moccasins and a blanket. The women wore long loose dresses, wide leather belts studded with brass tacks, and moccasins. For head covering a woman used a handkerchief. A blanket also completed her wardrobe. If pants were bought by an Indian, the legs were cut off and a breached cloth worn with them. If a hat were used its crown was cut away for the purpose of letting in the air. Boots of any description were never worn by either sex.

"Sometimes a prominent head man would issue invitations to other leading men for a social evening. At these gatherings the usual custom was followed of smoking from a huge pipe passed around at intervals, and storytelling.

"About the only industry among the Indians at that time was the raising of large pony herds, in which some succeeded very well. A few years later the Indian Department decided to try and encourage stock raising by my people and a system of trading horses for cattle was introduced. This resulted in a number of Indians owning fair sized herds of cattle which they sold to the Indian Department for rationing purposes. All monies derived from such sales were credited to the individual Indian at the agency. Wagons and farm implements then began to make their appearance among the Indians. Hay cutting time would see long lines of hay racks filled with hay moving in the direction of a nearby town. This hay was sold for Mounted Police requirements of various police detachments.

---

[160] Unfortunately, like many non-Indian farms, these fields today are planted and harvested by large absentee corporations.

"Considerable progress too, was made by the different churches in persuading the Indians to change their faith. Numerous adults in our reserve were baptized and confirmed. Two from the Blackbird reserve actually stood up in a church pulpit several times and preached the gospel message.

"Schools were administered by different religious denominations. Pupils attended the schools up to the age of 18 when they were discharged and returned to reserves. Some of these ex-pupils became successful in the lines which they studied at these educational institutions. I attended the Calgary Indian Industrial School[161], built exclusively for Indian boys from various reserves in Western Canada. This great educational centre taught its pupils carpentry, farming, printing, and the bakery trade. These proved especially useful to many of the students graduated from that school.

Calgary Indian Industrial School
(Now the intersection of Deerfoot and Glenmore Trails)

"In 1905, when I graduated, the Indians were still being fed by the government with rations of flour and meat being issued to us twice a week. But since my people have proved to the Indian Department that they could be self supporting, the system was abolished soon after. Rationing was then confined to older and invalided tribesmen.

---

[161] Mike was captain of the twenty-one-member soccer team at this school.

"Rubber tired buggies and democrats were common means of locomotion at this period, the travois having been discarded some years earlier. A few years later agricultural pursuits were encouraged by Department officials. Thousands of acres of land were sown to wheat and oats annually. Modern homes and community halls, replacing the primitive log structures which had served in the past, began to make their appearance. They were built entirely by Indians.

"The attitude of my people during World War One is sufficient proof of their right to be called British subjects. I defy anyone to cite a single instance of an Indian serving as a conscript in that war[162]. The Indian is a born warrio[163]r; it has always been a part of a brave to fight his enemies. Therefore, any legislation making it compulsory for a nation to fight a foreign foe would appear ludicrous in the eyes of the Indian.

"Further proof of the progress of my people during the past sixty years may be given in the following facts: by the 1930s our womenfolk no longer served as servile drudges; every Sunday the churches on the various reserves were filled with well-dressed Indian couples who, in most cases, drove to worship in modern, up-to-date cars, some equipped with radios. Some of our young ladies were serving as qualified registered nurses[164] in many of the hospitals throughout Canada.

"It has been a hard struggle, I must admit, for those who have helped us in the past. Still, **I think some credit is due my people for the advancement made.** We are not looking forward to the time the buffalo shall return[165]. Nor are we anticipating a time when the white man shall disappear from the continent. But we are scanning the horizon for further chances of advancement and further opportunities of proving ourselves true and loyal subjects of the British Empire."

---

[162] As the War carried on, volunteers were insufficient to fill depleted ranks, so the Canadian Government had to implement conscription to meet their "commonwealth quota", which caused protest riots in Quebec. "Indian Affairs estimated that 4,000 First Nations men enlisted [voluntarily]. These records are incomplete ..... and don't include non-Status Indians and Métis." (CBC Radio, Indigenous veterans: They fought for freedom, democracy, and an equality they could never share, November 11, 2018.)

[163] "The Blackfoot were a warlike nation, proud and fiercely independent." Alex, Johston and den Otter, *Lethbridge A Centennial History*, 1985, page 23.

[164] My aunt Belle served as a registered nurse in the Royal Canadian Air Force during the Second World War.

[165] Mike is being sarcastic here.

True and loyal subjects of the British Empire is more of the public attitude of Mike's time than the outlook of the Indian. This is noteworthy because Mike is merely reflecting a non-Indian, and mostly official, position and is saying what he thinks others want to hear, not what he feels. I doubt any Indian wanted "opportunities of proving ourselves true and loyal subjects of the British Empire".

One can share Mike's remorse about "so called civilization extinguish [ing] my people from the face of the earth". However, the extinction might not be from the reasons he discusses. Certainly, almost all major health indicators put the health of the current Indian population below that of the non-Indian population, but one might speculate as to why this is so. Most emphatically it is not the non-Indians fault nor is it their responsibility. It is time Indians took responsibility for their own success or failure, and not always crying fiduciary rights as a source for their demands for more money.

All of modern medicine and health care available to non-Indians is available to Indians, so why are Indians so less healthy[166]. Could it be because they do not have a regular exercise routine, or active lifestyle, like working for instance? I know Indians that had the opportunity to work in different projects but held that they did not want jobs, they wanted dividends; and I suppose that is what they get when they have non-Indians work Indian land. They get the dividends, but they do not get the exercise. Plus Treaty money and cash for things like *Truth & Reconciliation* from taxpayers who did nothing to people that it did not happen to.

If anything is going to lead to the extinction of Mike's people, it is going to be inactivity; we are killing them with kindness, providing everything they ask for without any effort from them[167].

---

[166] Data to support this assertion is consistent and affirmed by Indians' continuous demands for more health care, among other things.

[167] A senior civil servant in Ottawa said to me: "Indians think they can come to Ottawa and get money any time they want. Indians can pound sand".

The last time I saw Mike

The last time I saw Mike was in the old two story, wood frame hospital building on the north edge Cardston. I had been visiting him, having been alerted that his life was ending.

After walking away down the narrow hallway, I felt his eyes on me so I stopped, and turned to look back at him. He was sitting on the edge of his bed, wearing only a snow-white hospital night shirt, his black legs dangling from a high bed.

A long look at each other, and then a smile from him that seemed to create a glow. At that moment, I thought of all the changes in the world he had experienced, from a kid growing up in a teepee to a world war survivor to a solid Canadian citizen and writer and public speaker. He was an admirable example of integration without cultural assimilation.

Seeing his smile, I hoped that I could be like Mike Mountain Horse, laughing like he did when he was called a dirty old Indian. I wanted to smile at the end and see, enjoy and understand the big changes that had occurred in the world during my lifetime, as he had in his; hanges like computers and space travel, among many others. On the personal level, the biggest change has been lifestyle and standard of living, including the introduction of birth control, probably the most significant social change ever in North America with the upheaval in the male/female equation; and the continuous and expanding improvement in education and its more democratic accessibility at higher levels.

Finally though, it is how our individual lives are affected, or determined, day to day, that concerns everyone the most.

Mike's grave site

Cemeteries are interesting footnotes to local history.[168]

A high school summer job I had was cutting the grass at the Lethbridge cemetery that was surrounded by many poplar trees which sheltered its own secure and serene spot in the world. A small crew of about ten kept the grounds as trim and proper as a child being sent off to school for the first day. Only two of the crew were entrusted to dig the graves though, and they did so with a small well-worn stick of about two and a half feet that they manipulated to precisely measure the width, length, and depth of a new grave. The walls of the finished graves were as precise and smooth as though they had been poured with concrete.

The cemetery had modest headstones (tombstones) that if vandalized by boozing teenagers were quickly repaired or replaced. From time to time, some young people thought it brazen if they did it there in the dark, much like those folks who think it to be a big laugh to join the "mile high club", a bonus of the inexpensive jet age.

The Arlington military cemetery in Washington is so large and so meticulously, reverently, maintained, with monuments marking major, significant moments in American history, that it is impossible for one visiting it to remain unmoved, the imagery of ranks of combatants that somehow becomes just one fallen person forlornly standing resolutely before time, underlining the dictum "we shall never forget".

Looking over the thousands of graves one not only highly and unequivocally respect those who lay there but also reminds us to reflect on our responsibility, or our failure, to prevent the reason they died; the one undeniable reason, war, our inability as people to live peacefully together.

After a prolonged pensive introspection, my eyes focused on the headstone immediately before me. It was for an actor I recalled mentioned by Mike Mountain Horse, a mostly cowboy actor whose movies were like *40 Guns to Apache Pass* or *Apache Rifles,* a source of mirth to Mike, reflected in his use of the word "paleface" to disparage the idea

---

[168] Of course you wouldn't want to overstay your visit.

that cowboys never missed when shooting at an Indian but that Indians could never hit anything.[169]

The cemeteries in New Orleans are very elaborate because they are mostly above ground. The water level is too high to bury people, or putting it another way, much of the city is below sea level, which became very obvious when hurricane Katrina burst the levées and the city was flooded, and one result was coffins floating away[170]. The tombs become communal over time because space for new tombs is unavailable, so tombs had shelves for new arrivals. They have become a must-see for tourists to the city.

I think that Jack Nicolson or Dennis Hopper or Peter Fonda (son of Henry Fonda, a more well-known Hollywood actor) did it there in the movie *Easy Rider*. When I was in that cemetery, I tried to find the spot, but could not. A quote from Jack Nicholson's character was "Neh! Neh! Fuh! Fuh! Indians", whatever that is supposed to mean, although I cannot imagine it was flattering, but I wonder if political correctness would have permitted it to be included in the movie if it was made in 2020 instead of 1969.

I visited a deserted and remarkably interesting graveyard in the centre of Prague, Czech Republic. It is the size of a city lot in Calgary and has about a ten-foot wall. Over the years, people were buried on top of each other, or layered with the addition of soil, so that each grave is characterized by several markers. Over time, the level of the graveyard came to be meters higher than the surrounding street, so the wall was built as a retaining wall.

It is a Jewish cemetery, started before Columbus discovered the new world. Right away, the issue of discrimination comes to mind. However, there is another way one might look at this, and that is in

---

[169] The actor was Audie Murphy, who was the most decorated American in World War II. He "received every military combat award for valor available from the U.S. Army [including the nation's highest award, the Medal of Honor]" as well as decorations from France and Belgium.

More than an actor, he exuded a sincere and humble personality, which was obvious from the look in his eyes and the way his shoulders were bunched in his autobiographical movie titled To Hell and Back, a Hollywood depiction of his war exploits and a source of much embarrassment for Mr Murphy. While stationed in North Africa, his squad included an Indian whom they called "Chief" and one "who smokes cigars a lot".

[170] New Orleans "a city several feet below sea level ….. they saw corpses float by." The New Times, Remembering Katrina [Hurricane Katrina, August 2005] , August 23, 2020.

reverse: maybe the Jews wanted to be buried separate from others. It is known that many of the early eastern European settlements of Jews (shtetls) were located outside towns because of Jewish initiatives, not that they were exiled or expelled by local town residents. One of the reasons for the distancing was differences in the sanitary knowledge, the Jewish practices being more advanced than those in the townsites.

Another graveyard I have visited, this one by accident, was near Tallinn, Estonia. It was in a wooded area, in a ravine that was partly flooded, swamp-like. Monuments and iron railings were crumbling and rumpled. There was no road into the site, nothing to mark it. It was hard not to conclude, given the European and Nazi history of the area, that this disrespected burial site was Jewish.

Discrimination by any name.

Now, let us talk about Mike Mountain Horse's grave site, wherever it may be. I called the Kainai administration building asking where his grave was. I finally was connected

20 Old Jewish cemetery in Prague

with one whose federally funded job was trying to find the names of those in graves on the reserve. He was doing this pursuant to the *Truth and Reconciliation Program* of the Canadian Government. My inquiry was timely, he said, because they were using GPS to find and name graves so they could measure the extent of the residential school disgrace, which he asserted was broad because "thousands" of children had died in the schools. Consulting his database, he confidently said there was a monument to Mike at the cemetery on the Belly River, near the north end of the Reserve close to McLeod. Come down and I'll show it to you, and then I'll buy you lunch in Fort Mcleod. He suggested ten in the morning next Wednesday. Okay, see you then.

However, I have dealt with Indians too much over the years to take them at their word. One time I was picked up by an Indian team to play with them in a basketball tournament. Every game started at least an hour late. So, for the championship game, I decided to arrive late. For this game, they had started early and finished before I got there.

Another time, at the Indians' request, I had arranged a meeting with an environmental expert from Ottawa. After travelling from

Ottawa, the expert and I arrived at a mostly empty Indian administration building. The purpose of the meeting was to discuss the progress of a Canadian Government sponsored project in Panama to have the Indians, who had experience finding and removing unexploded ordinance, show the Panamanians how to do it. In the end, the missed meeting did not matter. The Indians who were sent by Ottawa to Panama would not get out of their five-star Panama hotel and used the time to spend their per diems on what many would consider undesirable. The Panamanian government project leader called me and apologetically said they would like me to come back to their country any time, but please do not bring those Indians with you.

So, I had little confidence that the Kainai guide would show up, never mind knowing where Mike's grave was. I was at Mike's burial, and it was not on the north end of the Kainai reserve: it was on the south end. With a Plan B in mind I left Calgary for the Reserve.

There is a road from Coalhurst, just ten kilometers north of Lethbridge, that runs west across the Kainai reserve for about 45 minutes to Standoff, the location of the Kainai administration building where I was to meet my guide to Mike's grave. Along the way, there are numerous reserve residences, most not larger than Atco trailers with a satellite dish and two vehicles parked alongside and surrounded by rich, golden wheat fields waiting to be harvested, but no sign of farm equipment or machinery to do the work. That is because most, if not all, of the Indians do not work the land, the Tribe leases it to non-Indians and the Tribe earns revenue.

This is good business because non-Indian corporate farmers plant and harvest with great efficiency, which they have to do because the lease is fixed, straight take or pay; the lease does not change with low crop yields due to unfavorable weather or low prices due to depressed world markets. This reminds me of playing golf in Bangkok where the caddies are all small women carrying golf bags that are almost as big as them. Although one might feel sorry for them, I thought health-wise in the long run they benefitted more than the golfers because they were getting exercise while the golfers were not[171].

---

[171] But this is not unlike golfers in Canada who ride in little carts while playing golf. I asked a golf partner (Steve Sparks), both of us walking and carrying our clubs, why these men younger than us were riding in carts. His answer was they were practicing being old.

Even though Indians were getting money by letting non-Indians do their work, I felt Indians were missing the development of skills and health benefits. Poor health statistics on reserves compared to the general Canadian population support casual observations.

I was disappointed my guide did not show up. I wanted to be proven wrong. Anyway, I drove off alone to where I knew Mike was buried, or at least I thought I did. The graveyard was a mess and so overgrown with weeds and unattended graves that I could not find his. Most wooden markers were rotten and fallen; headstones were crumbling and hidden by weeds. There was little to show that this was hallowed ground for revered ancestors. There were no pathways or rows of graves to show a pattern. Only a rutted trail through the middle with no regard for those who lay around, or beneath, it.

Acknowledging that I am generalizing but feeling the need to compare, it is easy to say of the cemeteries described, Lethbridge – respected; New Orleans – ornate; Arlington – meticulous; Prague – desperate; Tallinn – despairing; and, Kainai – forgotten.

Discussing this with one informed, I am told that maybe Indians have a way of looking at death that is different than a non-Indian.[172] Indians, it is said, feel that at death the spirit leaves the body, and the remains are not important. Probably some Indians, and non-Indians believe this, but compare the cemetery of a coastal Indian tribe (page 135) to the cemetery of Mike Mountain Horse (page 134). The coastal Indian cemetery is well marked and cared for.

Obviously not all Indians think alike, but it is hard for a non-Indian not to conclude that coastal Indians think more reverently of their ancestors than the Kanai Indians. Of course, I am being judgmental, but It is what it is, and it is this way because that must be the way they want it to be. By non-Indian standards, it is pathetic, but by Indian standards, it is the way the Indians want it.

Who am I to judge, but do not retort that things are the way they are because of racial discrimination, or because of the way Indians have

---

[172] Indian burial underground was not traditional. It began with the Christian Missionaries. Before then, burials were lodge or house burial, or tree or platform burial. Indian neglect of cemeteries therefore might be attributed to disrespect for white customs. (Ibid, Johnston and den Otter, page 23)

been treated. It is their cemetery; they have made it what is. They can clean it up, the non-Indian way, by Indian volunteers.

Do not expect me to pay for another Indian welfare project to find, mark, and clean up their cemeteries.

Grandfathers are heroes to every child, I do not apologize for that. Nor do I apologize for telling it like it is when talking about Indians. What I do is challenge every Indian to make sure that their grandchildren talk about them the way I talk about Mike Mountain Horse ….. a Canadian Hero.

21 Mike's cemetery, 2020

(There is nothing to indicate this is a cemetery)

22 West coast Indian cemetery

PART II THE WAY ITS GOING

One has to wonder if Indigenous people have a future given how their leaders continuously lament their lower standard of living. They could be describing an endangered species. If this continues, they might bear in mind, endangered often ends in extinct species, which might occur if they do not join the modern world instead of trying to use their culture as a reason not to.

Laying the blame for their plight on the Government does not help. It will have more structural issues to deal with over the coming years the small voting block that is Indigenous.

Over a hundred years of throwing money at the "Indian problem" has not solved the problem. That has recently been proven by the need for and the hundreds of millions of dollars spent on *Truth & Reconciliation*.

Many experts say *The Indian Act* is the problem, but the years trying to live within it has only complicated the problem. It is too easy to say abolish the *Act*, treat Indigenous as Canadians. Trying to unravel the Indian problem has frustrated so many they throw their hands in the air and just walk away – que será, será. Resort to the courts is only a short-term conciliation regardless of how much money is awarded and spent.

It is time for Indigenous to be Canadian. They are kept separate by treating them separate. For example, having a separate *Remembrance Day* for Indigenous people or "Indigenizing"[173] Mount Royal

---

[173] "The University has committed to a path toward Indigenization … efforts are evident in the classroom, where instructors and elders-in-residence are incorporating invaluable indigenous knowledge and ways of knowing into teachings from literature to physics and from geography to botany."

March 4, 2024, https://www.innovatingcanada.ca/diversity-and-inclusion/diversity-inclusion-archive/at-mount-royal-university-in-calgary-education-is-being-indigenized/#:~:text=in%20calgary%2C%20alberta%2C%20the%20campus%20of%20mount%20royal,and%20decolonization%20that%E2%80%99s%20redefining%20higher%20education%20in%20canada.

["Indigenous knowledge and ways of knowing" is not going to help an airplane mechanic or a Canada Arm developer. What will help is learning to function in the modern world rather than to retreat to the past.]

University is the same racial discrimination Canada has been denouncing for decades.

It is time for de-Indigenization of government and institutions, . It is government that encompasses and perpetuates discrimination. There is no better place to start than *The Indian Act*. Canadians can not say "Indian" because it may offend Indians. But the government can say Indians — *The INDIAN Act*.

"May the sun and the truth shine everywhere"

Alberta never joined CANADA.

Albertans in general, or those who lived here at the time (1905), Indian or non-Indian, were never asked if they wanted to join CANADA.

CANADA created *Alberta* in 1905 to serve the needs and interests of eastern CANADA. A good illustration of this is that when *Alberta* was created, ownership of *Alberta*'s natural resources (including oil and gas) where retained by CANADA, as compared to the eastern provinces retaining ownership of their natural resources.

In other words, from day one, *Alberta* was a second-class province. This more than anything demonstrates eastern Canada's ingrained attitude towards the west.

And if it was not natural resources, it was fodder for the First World War. Mike Mountain Horse and his brothers Albert and Joe gave their share in Europe's War. They left an isolated corner of southwestern *Alberta*, an obscure, peaceful un-noticed remote patch of the world, to be killed or kill for what the recruiting posters at the time shouted out "For King and Country".[174]

Really. For whose king and whose country? Returning to CANADA, Mike was denied, because he was an Indian, the veterans' benefits non-whites received. After that and years of continuous employment and resident in Lethbridge he was called the dirty old Indian.

I wonder if he ever questioned which was worse — the bullets and explosions or the pejoratives.

Whichever, it did not stop him from becoming a highly regarded and honoured man. He lived and spent his career in a non-Indian community; was a sought-after public speaker; wrote articles for newspapers and magazines. Schools requested his visits; a modern school in Lethbridge was named after him. He supported Mary Mountain Horse who had lost all her Treaty rights when she left the reserve because she was female, and her five children.

---

[174] A call to action still used in World War II as recorded in a war propaganda movie named "Captain of the Clouds" starring James Cagney. The movie is about brave Canadian bush pilots being recruited to fly bombers for the English. Its main filming location was Ottawa.

His Story Robe about his War battles is in two museums (the original in the *Medicine Hat Esplanade*, a copy in *The Military Museums of Calgary*. For a time, the original was in the *Canadian Military Museum*).

The land of Mike's youth is still there, the undulating brown prairie grassland with gentle knolls to the *Porcupine Hills* at the foothills of the *Rocky Mountains*, a wall to everything west except the winter Chinook winds that change buffalo-robe freezing weather into buckskin warm days; the winds that loudly bull their way through the treetops lining the creeks and streams. And, it was empty land during Mike's lifetime, freeing him to wander alone and lazily ponder the stories told by huge clouds that had no regard for the observer, so far below and small.

Roaming that prairie, it must have seemed as vast to a horse rider as the ocean was to a sailor; and his course as uncertain as that of the sailor who depended on the direction of the wind. It is hard to know, let alone imagine, what thoughts Mike had at those times, but certainly they were simple compared to the complexity of modern life, limited to only those things around him that he had experienced in his small world.

But it is not hard to imagine his thoughts when he came back from the War. His mind was now filled with experiences of trains, oceans, people in ships, cities, and trenches. And all manners of shell broken body parts lying about.

Understandingly or not, when he returned to his prairie homeland, he committed to treasuring it and those around him; and to not forgetting that commitment for one day for the rest of his life. And that is how he lived to the day he died in 1964:

"May the sun and the truth shine everywhere"

Canada as a MacDonald's franchise

Alberta in 1964 was much different than it had been when it was created in 1905, the year my father arrived as an infant by horse and cart from Iowa. In 1930, the Federal Government transferred to *Alberta* the ownership of natural resources within the province. In 1947, large commercial reserves of oil were found near Leduc, the production and export of which elevated *Alberta* from a purely agrarian community to a world class economic and financial engine that gave *Alberta*ns one of the highest standards of living in the world.

This was great to have, but it also brought with it unwanted problems much like those that lottery winners have – that is, more friends and relatives the lottery winners knew they had. In *Alberta*'s case, the new-found friend was the Federal Government requesting, then taking, a "fair share" of the oil revenue "for all Canadians". That fair share would have to come from what the Federal Government considered excess profit but which the *Alberta* Government saw as savings for future generations, given that oil was a depleting, non-renewable resource.

This fair share was not much of a public issue until the price of oil rose to unprecedented levels. It rose to these prices because the *Organization of Petroleum Exporting Countries* (OPEC) used its majority share of world production to charge a "political" price that was unrelated to the cost of production. The political price, far above the cost of production, was intended to punish those countries, primarily the U.S., for their support of Israel in the *Middle East* wars.

The Federal Government saw this political price as excess unearned profit and saw no reason for *Alberta* to be the sole beneficiary at the expense of Canadian consumers.

Game on, with two perfectly antagonistic players. Prime Minister Pierre Trudeau with a fixed national point of view, and Premier Peter Lougheed, with a *not on my turf provincial attitude*. If the two could be characterized as football players, Lougheed was a head down, straight ahead blocker, whatever the play called for. His was what is called a strength position.

Trudeau would be a skilled position player with a general sense of where the ball or the game was going and a green light to whatever came instinctively.

Canada is like a MacDonald's Hamburger franchise: franchisees (the provinces) making the hamburgers and the franchisor (central government) making the rules for the franchisees and taking whatever share of the profits it likes.

The central government does not cut timber, does not catch fish, does not grow wheat, does not plant potatoes, does not mine zinc, does not manufacture cars. What it does is take a cut of all provincial production and in return gives the franchisees the right to erect a big patented, Canadian golden arch outside its business doors.

And given the success of the Macdonald's arches around the world, there is nothing wrong with that – something Quebec and Alberta separatist should keep in mind.

That is the advantage of having an international brand called CANADA.

English colonialism in CANADA receded, it did not abruptly end. Some feel that the end began in 1917 at Vimy Ridge in World War I where Mike Mountain Horse was wounded two times) and ended in 1931 when the statute of Westminster made the *Supreme Court of Canada* the final court of appeal in 1949, instead of the English *Judicial Committee of the Privy Council.*

However, this was not the end. *The British North America Act* of 1867 (BNA) that served as Canada's constitution was still an act of the English Parliament and therefore could be amended only by the English Parliament[175]. Canadians could not amend it, and therefore did not have total control of their own destiny, which was, with the displays of Quebec separation, shaky.

---

[175] This is like *The Indian Act*, which is an act of Canada's Parliament and thus its right alone to amend ... or abolish, without consulting anyone.

The end of colonialism

English colonialism in CANADA receded, it did not abruptly end. Some feel that the end began in 1917 at Vimy Ridge in World War I where Mike Mountain Horse was wounded two times) and ended in 1931 when the statute of Westminster made the *Supreme Court of Canada* the final court of appeal in 1949, instead of the English *Judicial Committee of the Privy Council.*

However, this was not the end. *The British North America Act* of 1867 (BNA) that served as Canada's constitution was still an act of the English Parliament and therefore could be amended only by the English Parliament[176]. Canadians could not amend it, and therefore did not have total control of their own destiny, which was, with the displays of Quebec separation, shaky.

Until Quebec, that staunch objector to all things Canadian, lit a fire under Canadians[177]. In a 1980 referendum, the Quebec Government unsuccessfully sought a mandate from its voters to separate from Canada. The Government tried again in 1995 and lost by only a statistically negligible 0.58 %. Both referendums got people's attention.

Prime Minister Pierre Trudeau just resurrected from the politically dead, saw the Quebec challenge as an opportunity to do that personal thing he had be trying to do for a decade, and failed — patriate[178] the *BNA* — and now he resolutely set out to do that as he had nothing to lose, and to hell with everything and anyone else, which of course got premiers sputtering "not on my watch".

During this same time the Canadian and *Alberta* governments were locked in a decade long battle over the revenue from oil sales, the federal government's position being that it was its purpose to spread this wealth equally over CANADA while the *Alberta* Government's position was simple – we own it, which it did pursuant to the federal *Natural Resources Transfer Act* of 1930. To underline this point, *Alberta* decreased the oil supply to eastern CANADA by 15%, which did nothing but

---

[176] This is like *The Indian Act*, which is an act of Canada's Parliament and thus its right alone to amend … or abolish, without consulting anyone.

[177] In a recent blog from Moscow, a young man was being interviewed. He objected to being introduced as a Canadian. "I'm from Quebec" he said. " Canada is our enemy".

[178] Transfer control of the constitution (the ultimate authority of a nation) from the mother country to its former colony.

reduce Alberta's share of revenue from its oil production. Eastern CANADA simply increased imports of oil from AFRICA and VENEZUELA.

Trudeau was non-pulsed since he knew in the end he would win because the *BNA* deck was stacked in his favor — the federal government had the authority to write the rules in regard to taxation. His problem was he did not control the game's end date, and if this was prolonged too long, he would lose the momentum, or be un-elected again or die, before he could ram through the patriation of the BNA. He therefore compromised with the provinces, principally Premier Lougheed of *Alberta,* who was applying pressure with his rigid control of oil supply.

Trudeau paid a high price, however, for the compromise. The price was a "notwithstanding" clause[179] in the *Canadian Charter of Rights and Freedoms* that Trudeau had stuck on the bottom of the BNA to be patriated. The BNA was simply an administrative document, the Charter gave CANADA a heart and soul, and this was Trudeau's vision, for which he will be rightly revered in the future, long after all his contemporary, quibbling self-interested premiers are gone.

Many see the "notwithstanding clause" as the beginning of" ten little countries" rather than one united country. The clause has the potential of creating different rights and freedoms in each province.

This not what Mike Mountain Horse lived for (*A Mike Mountain Message for Canad*a, page 12)

---

[179] The notwithstanding clause enables provinces that wish to, to enact over-riding legislation on certain parts of the *Charter*, something Quebec (who else) has done with every single piece of its legislation since patriation of the BNA in 1982. This makes one wonder how Quebec would do in a national referendum on Quebec's membership in Canada.

What Mike fought for

Mike Mountain Horse's motto was: (Page 139)

"May the sun and the truth shine everywhere"[180]

Mike fought for his country and his people. Following is an example of his writing in which he fights for his people:

Letter to the Calgary Herald, December 12, 1925:

The Piegan Indian Lease

I am writing a letter in the hope of laying down a few facts before the public concerning the recent Indian convention in Macleod

Now. Mr. Editor, why did the Indians go into convention? I will answer the question: because we thought fit to remind the Dominion government that they have broken their treaty with us, that was made in 1877, by passing an amendment to the Indian Act, whereby they can lease Indian reserves against the vote of the Indian.

These Indian reserves were set aside for us by the Treaty of 1877 to be the property of the Indians forever, and today we find the Dominion Government leasing these reserves to political friends, as has been done on the Piegan reserve.

I will answer certain letters that appeared in the papers. I will take that of A.J. McLean first: Mr. McLean. says there is only one family interested in the Piegan lease, and that this family was entirely satisfied when their claim was properly adjusted. Mr. McLean knows that this is not well founded. He knows there are about eleven other families in that area which the Dominion Government has very kindly let him have for the high price of $0.06 per acre, per annum, when the lowest that the Peigan Indians asked for such lease was $0.15 per acre, and there

---

[180] Burkitt, Thyrza, *Indian Soldier Recalls Pioneer Days*, Calgary Herald, December 26, 1936.

was never a charge at the Indian convention that certain hay on the Piegan Reserve had disappeared, as I was present all the time of the convention. Mr. McLean also says that this lease was applied for to the Indian commissioner in the usual way, and that customary procedure was followed in every respect.

I do not think it is the customary procedure to pick out the choicest pieces of grazing land that the Indians have for themselves, when the Indian Act says that the superintendent-general of Indian affairs may lease any portion of the Indian reserve, without the consent of the Indians, If the band was neglecting to cultivate or make use of the said land. There are two Indians farming in that area, on a small scale and the other in his own way, while the balance of the land was used by families for pasture.

Mr McLean has gone to work and fenced them in, and today they have a very small area for their stock Section 49 says that no release or surrender of any Indian reserve shall be binding unless assented to by a majority of the band, and there is no such thing in the Indian Act as a permanent release such as quoted by Mr. McLean, who also says that Mister Coates assertions are false when he says that the lease was granted against the will of the Indians. I have a letter from Commissioner Graham of the Indian department, to show that the Piegan reserve lease was granted against the will of Indians. This will prove that Mister Coote was correct, and the fact is true that not one Peigan Indian knew that his land was leased to Mr. McLean for 10 years.

I have evidence to prove all this true, also about the one man being satisfied when his claim was properly adjusted. I have this from the Indian himself.

He was paid $40 for his house, stable, roothouse, pasture fence, besides his oats and potatoes, which were destroyed, since he was ordered to stay away from his home, which his widowed mother has tried for 10 years to build up. $40 is not her claim, but $250 for her home and claim. Today they are living in a tent, for the property belonged to her, not to her son, to whom Mr. McLean paid the huge sum of$40.

I will, answer Mr. White's letter next week, when my reports come in and hope you will be kind enough to post that also.

The Government of Canada made a treaty with my people in 1877. They gave us reserves forever, and passed an amendment 1918 whereby they can lease our reserves without our consent, breaking the great Treaty of 1877. The government of Canada went to war on account of a treaty being broken, and here we find them doing the same thing at home. If there is such a thing as British justice, I hope the public will get behind the Indians and demand that these leases, which were put through under this amended Act, will be declared null and void and the land restored to the Indians.

On behalf of my Indians …. MIKE MOUNTAIN HORSE

Indigenous fixated on the past miss the future

In the First World War, Mike Mountain Horse would have been an officer and decorated for valour, instead of an acting sergeant and given just a *Distinguished Conduct Medal*.

Most Indian arguments are with the future, using events from the past as justification that resonate with only a small portion of the general population. The arguments, although understood, have very little non-Indian support, and, as time goes by, will have even less as the world that surrounds Indians, like it or not, moves on.

So, the only practicable option for them is to join the world or be left behind, to become extinct, as will happen if the Canadian Government keeps killing them with largess. Insisting on educating their young in their native language and culture will be of no use to their teenage daughters trying to order, in one or another of their close to one hundred languages and dialects, a Slurpy in the local Seven-Eleven. As well it is most likely they will be served in English by those for whom English is not their first language; and it is highly likely they ae being served in English by some who's first language is something else.

Mike Mountain Horse successfully joined the modern world while keeping his cultural heritage. He was honoured by the non-Indian community of Lethbridge that named a school after him; and a copy of his wartime story robe is in the *Calgary Military Museum* (page 215).

His Indian society made him an honorary chief while renaming him *Mike Crossing Many Rivers*, recognizing his many travels.

Many of us, Indian or non-Indian, would do well to emulate Mike's life. However, in one way, we failed terribly. He fought in the "War to end all Wars", but in a little more than twenty years later, the world was at war again. That Second World War ended in one of history's worst single massacres with the explosion of atomic bombs over two cities in Japan[181]. Radioactive fallout from the plant building one of those bombs at Hanford, Washington, just south of Mike's birthplace, eventually settled on Mike's grave in the southwest corner of *Alberta*.

Face it, prejudices are inherently human, and no amount of legislating is going to change that. Playing basketball in Calgary, players coming off the floor ask "who are you checking" and in the absence of any other identifying feature, the answer may just be "the black guy", or "the old" guy. No offense play on. Calgary's official web site talks about "Calgary Chinatown Residency", or "Tomorrow's Chinatown". No problem, plan on.

In Port of Spain two uniformed black presidential guards poked me in the chest with their M-14 rifles because I was white and asked, "you want to die Mon". Okay, no harm no foul, just move on. In Bangkok, an old woman half of a mom and pop pineapple street vendor loudly chews out her husband for cheating me with my change. Thank you, lady, I will not forget your consideration. In the Thai *National Petroleum Building* down the street, two engineers block my entrance to an otherwise empty elevator and tell me to take the next one. Sure, we will see you upstairs.

Everybody experiences personal discrimination of one kind or another: red hair, gender, clothing, ethnicity, race, too old, too young, too tall, too short, too heavy, too thin, almost anything visible. More pernicious though than personal discrimination is systemic discrimination that is embedded within our society, and there is no more gross example of that than the Indian Act. The Indian Act is a law of our Canadian Parliament and it perpetuates this discrimination in the *Charter of Rights and Freedoms* (Section 25 – Aboriginal and Treaty Rights).

Regardless of the long out-of-date reasons for Indian rights, they are no longer appropriate for a modern CANADA. In the *Charter*, there are no rights for Italians or Ukrainians or Chinese or Japanese, or whatever. There are only rights for Canadians, and it's about time Indians

---

[181] Hiroshima and Nagasaki.

had the same rights; or, if that is too hard to grasp then change the Constitution, so everybody has only Indian rights.

To start, abolish the Indian Act, which the Parliament of Canada can do because it created the act. This will eliminate Indians, and we will have only Canadians left. Canadian parliamentarians have tried to do this for decades, but Indians have blocked them from doing so. So Indians, if you are serious about putting a big spike into systematic discrimination, get rid of the legislation that defines your discrimination – it brands you as different and that trickles down through all other legislation and laws that affect you.

To compensate for anything left on the balance books for Indians, the Canadian Government could transfer title to the land defined as reservations, although many would argue that Indians have already been overcompensated (footnote 3).

Furthermore, all Indian specific programs should be eliminated, or amended to include all other Canadians. True equality, end discrimination; it is time, and necessary, for Indians to earn some self-respect and become Canadians.

If Alberta had won the oil war

The Oil War began the day in 1905 that *Alberta* was created a province by eastern CANADA. The four provinces of eastern CANADA each kept ownership of natural resources within their boundaries when CANADA was formed in 1867. However the Federal Government kept ownership of *Alberta*'s natural resources when *Alberta* was created.

Thus, CANADA became comprised of two tiers of provinces: a first-class tier (Ontario, Quebec, Nova Scotia, and New Brunswick), and a second-class tier (Manitoba, Saskatchewan, and *Alberta*). This did not go unnoticed in the prairie provinces. Why, they complained and argued over the years, did the eastern provinces own the natural resources within their boundaries and the prairies did not?

To the eastern provinces this was not a matter of any concern. After all, the prairies were created by and colonized for, that is exploited, for their eastern progenitors. What could be more natural than that?

Well, from a modern point of view, equal status among provinces might be more natural, the prairies stressed, to which the Federal Government finally agreed and passed a series of acts titled *The Natural Resources Transfer Act* in 1931. This Act gave ownership of natural resources to each of the western provinces.[182]

However, during *Alberta*'s oil war with Ottawa, Premier Lougheed of *Alberta* always spoke about the "ownership of our natural resources", specifically oil, implying that the Federal Government was stealing *Alberta*'s oil. Lougheed knew that this not the case, but in the public media battle between himself and Trudeau, he knew it was easier

---

[182] The act in the series that is specifically for Alberta is titled Alberta Natural Resources Act, 1930.

The purpose of the Act was to place Alberta "in a position of equality with other provinces of Confederation .... [and] ..... In order that the Province may be in the same position as the original Provinces of Confederation, the interest of the Crown in all Crown lands, mines, minerals (precious and base) and royalties derived therefrom within the Province .... and all sums due or payable for such lands, mines, minerals or royalties, ... shall, from and after the coming into force of this agreement and subject as therein otherwise provided, belong to the Province ....". [Alberta Natural Resources Act, S.C., c.3, Memorandum of Agreement made this fourteenth day of December, 1929, Section 1]

to communicate, and for *Alberta*ns to understand, simple ownership. In fact, the issue was taxation, who got what share of the revenue from oil sales, not ownership, and Trudeau understood this and was patient because over time, the federal government's legislation was paramount and thus would get the share it wanted, one way or another.

In the end, after a decade of wrangling and bludgeoning *Alberta* with the *National Energy Program*, among other things, Lougheed signed an *Agreement* September 2, 1981, declared victory and went home, declaring that "the pact was a triumph for federalism".[183]

In any case, assessing the share of oil revenues pursuant to the *Agreement* compared to the *National Energy Program,* over the first five years of the *Agreement*, the Federal Government estimated that "Ottawa's share will rise from 24% to 29%, *Alberta*'s share will rise to 34% from 33%, and industry's share will drop from 43% to 33%"[184].

Alberta's change in revenue share is well inside a statistical rounding error — it did not change, which can hardly be called a victory for *Alberta*. The only way it could be called a victory is if a victory is defined as the status quo. The victor is clearly Trudeau and Ottawa at the expense of the oil industry.

The old adage of "you can't fight City Hall" comes to mind when thinking of Lougheed and *Alberta* against Trudeau and CANADA. You cannot win, the rules of the game are against you. The constitution trumped oil ownership. As Trudeau knew and Lougheed was not willing to accept was that it did not matter who owned the oil: what mattered was who held the tax hammer[185]. What grated Lougheed so much was

---

[183] I believe Lougheed's use of the word "federalism" as opposed to "confederation" was deliberate because being a premier and a lawyer, he would be well acquainted with the difference between the two words. This is a clear sign, if his action were not already, that his intended path was towards ten little countries, where the provinces held the ultimate power instead of the Federal Government).

[184] junewarren-nickles energy group, oilpatch history, *Trudeau, Lougheed Sign Agreement*, September 2, 1981.

As a footnote to the stick handling in the constitutional war and the role of the oil battle in it, it would be interesting to do a PhD thesis on the distribution of oil revenues over the lifetime of the oil fields.

[185] Constitution of Canada, The raising of Money by any mode or system of Taxation, Section 91, Subsection 3.

Trudeau condescendingly smiling at him as Trudeau brandished the hammer.

The development of oil reserves and its windfall profits turned *Alberta* from a placid agrarian based society into a world centre for wild-catters and a financial centre for CANADA. Large pools of money meant political power, something *Alberta* and the West coveted, and which the East would never let go. *Alberta*, recognizing that once oil was sucked out of the earth it could not be replanted like wheat in the Spring, tried to save some of the profit for future generations. Regrettably, the rest of CANADA saw this as profiteering and continuously let *Alberta* know how unCanadian this was, to the point where *Alberta*, tired of a history of being a colony to the east, said to the hell with it and decided to spend its oil savings.

A regrettable corollary of this oil development was an environ-mental calamity. Faced with the depletion of conventional oil reserves (the kind where you stick a iron straw into the ground and suck up the oil) and its associated decrease in revenue for government, *Alberta* urged, with tax incentives and favourable royalty schemes, the oil indus-try to mine oil (digging up oil sands with huge shovels and then like a sponge squeezing the oil out of the sand) before it had developed tech-nology to do so with environmental responsibility.[186]

Over almost half a century, the industry pumped out oil and the *Alberta* Government, along with a Federal Government, compliant be-cause it received huge tax revenue as well, accumulated large amounts

---

[186] An interesting footnote to the development of the oil sands. Premier Ernest Manning of Alberta "met with enthusiasm" a Richfield Oil Corporation's "scheme to deploy a nine-kiloton nuclear device in the bituminous sands of Fort McMurray" which would "double the world's petroleum reserves." The project was dropped, not because of health or en-vironmental concerns but because of worries about Russian spying. Vailant, John, *Fire Weather: The Making of a Beast*, 2003.

of money that it used for things that it would not otherwise have afforded[187].

---

[187] Edmonton Journal, Alberta's investments in the private sector have proven both rewarding and risky, April 11, 2018: MagCan (magnesium smelter, $164 million), NovaTel (cellphone manufacture, $614 million), Millar Western and Alberta-Pacific (pulp and paper, $422 million), Gainers (meat packing, $209), Swan Hills (hazardous waste treatment, $615 million), Kananaskis Golf Course (about $50 million). [Ibid, Morton and McDonald.]

"The Lougheed-Getty 'forced-growth' economic diversification projects are conservatively estimated to have cost Albertans $2.2 billion [about $1,000 per Alberta taxpayer]. While former premier Don Getty got most of the blame for these losses (as many came to light during his watch), most of these programs began earlier. Lougheed's push for government-led diversification of the Alberta economy …" [Ted Morton and Meredith McDonald, University of Calgary School of Public Policy, The Siren Song of Economic Diversification: Alberta's Legacy of Loss, Volume 8 Issue 13, March 2005.]

Indigenous share of oil windfall

While this scenario played out in the second half of the twentieth century and the beginning of the next millennium, *Alberta*'s Indian society, plagued by its own image problems, were docilely sequestered out there somewhere in the countryside, seldom seen except in parades for fairs and rodeos, for which they were paid a per diem and a bonus dependent upon the number of feathers in their native costumes. Meanwhile, aggressive Indian leaders, tired of chasing the Federal Government for more money needed for, they said, substandard education, poor health care, and inadequate housing, among other things, decided they were entitled to a larger share of the oil wealth, ultimately focused on civil disobedience to pursue their cause.

Aside from court actions conceived and designed by non-Indian consultants paid for by Canadian taxpayers that were usually based on either claims of non-consultation with Indians or environmental protection, the most widely noticed civil disobedience by Indians across Canada were railway blockades set up to stop the building of the *Coastal Gas Pipeline*. The pipeline had met all regulatory requirements and had the agreed support of 80% of the Indian tribes that lived anywhere on the planet close to where the pipeline was routed. However, a group of "hereditary chiefs", that is not elected like the others who had agreed to the pipeline route, announced that a spirit had motivated them to protect the land and therefore a pipeline could not be built. Non-Indian environmental activists jumped on this and recruited, and paid whoever they could to erect and man railroad blockades across the country, thus disrupting the Canadian supply chain and the economy it served. The Federal Government sat back and did nothing, thereby giving the blockaders the feeling they were winning and so could continue their illegal actions.

It took some *Alberta* roughnecks to put an end to that. With a truck they approached a newly erected blockade near Edmonton, loaded up the blockade, and drove away with it. No other attempt was made to build a blockade in *Alberta*. The Federal Government, fearing this bold assertion of public anger might encourage others in CANADA to do the same with the possibility of shoot-outs, decided to "negotiate" with the hereditary chiefs. An agreement was soon reached, partly because it was winter and blockaders were getting harder to find to sit out in the cold, but mostly because the Government promised more money for the Indians. How much money the Canadian public was not told and will not find out for more than a year until some industrious researcher filters through the public accounts.

Although the Indians got more cash, in the long term they face a loss of non-Indian support. Part of their protest included an invasion and occupation of the British Columbia Legislature.[188] Although generally sympathetic with Indian initiatives, the public has no tolerance for illegal activities like armed blockades and home invasions, which was what the occupation of the Legislature was.

No amount of cash is going to solve the Indian problem, for neither the Indians nor the Canadians that surround them.

---

[188] The amount of media attention and soul searching this received was minuscule compared to that of the invasion and occupation of the U.S. Capitol Building January 6, 2021.

Canada decaying country

CANADA must become sufficiently flexible to accommodate the ambitious mature demands of its regions and to demonstrate to those regions the benefits of being partners in a cooperative national relationship.

Canada' country "model" is archaic. Its structure cries for change as demonstrated by a Quebec referendum in 1995 that kept Canada together by a mere 0.58 percent! This fact is a *cri de coeur*, if not the sign of a crumbling country.

Alberta's decade long losing battle with Ottawa over oil is another obvious cry for change.

These and other cries for change are symptoms of the regions straining under the antiquated rules of confederation. The country must change to accommodate these long-term trends or ultimately suffer a breakup.

CANADA started as a confederation. That means it is the product of a large central power expanding and absorbing its surroundings, on the terms and rules of the central power. The residue of this is an inward-looking central power.

> *"The role of the federal government is to distribute wealth from the affluent to the disadvantaged. That was our policy for ..... regional equalization, and for energy."*[189]

The change CANADA needs is one that reflects a modern country directed by its components, the regions, reflecting the needs of the regions as opposed to predominantly those of just the central power. The structure of government intended to meet regional or provincial needs instead of a central government's needs, is a federal state, where the state serves the regions, instead of the other way around.

Premier Lougheed's crusade over Alberta's ownership "of our natural resources" inched us towards federation, whether the public

---

[189] Pierre Elliot Trudeau, Memoirs, 1993 page 295.

understood this or not. Inched because he knew that the oil battle was just that – a battle – in a long war against social inertia to change.

To carry the goal of federalism further, the provincial premeirs created the *Council of the Federation*, for which the plan is to "play a leadership role in the revitalizing the Canadian federation" [190].

The *Council of the Federation* has been projecting its members' interests by lobbying the American Government, as though the *Council* were representing the interests of Canada. For example, the *Council* attended the *2018 Summit [May 4-6] of North American Governors and Premiers,* ostensibly "to promote and advance cooperation by the leaders of the federated states of the world's most dynamic continent". In other words, the provinces in terms of authority were being accomodated as though they were American states.

In a mission to Washington (whatever and whoever that means) "the aim of the [Council] visit was to build and enhance relations with key American political leaders and to underscore Canadian contribu-tions to American security and prosperity".

The activities of the Council, if not ultra vires[191], clearly are pushing the envelope.

At the same time, Lougheed challenged the federal government by opening *Alberta* trade offices in Washington, Hong Kong, and Houston.[192]

---

[190] THE COUNCIL OF THE FEDERATION, *Canada's Premiers: Founding Agreement*, December 2003, https://www.canadaspremiers.ca/about/, June 12, 2020. I'll bet that 99.999% of Albertans do not know what this is, never mind even of hearing about it, although it has been around 18 years and has a staffed secretariat in Ottawa.

[191] Ultra viries is a term that referes to a federal or provincial action that is outsisde the authority allocated by the Constitution to either one government or the other. The constitutional authority of the Canadian Federal Government is generally "the Peace, Order, and Good Government of Canada in relation to all Matters not coming within the Classes of Subjects by this Act assigned exclusively to the Legislatures of the Provinces" [Powers of the Parliament, Section 91]. This sometimes is referred to as the residual powers. In The United States residual powers fall to the states.

The Exclusive Powers of Provincial Legislatures, Section 92, Subsection (16) are "Generally all Matters of a merely local or private Nature in the Province".

[192] The purpose of the offices had to be questioned when its head appointed to the Hou-ston office was Lougheed's haberdasher. But on the other hand, that was the only

Nevertheless, for Lougheed's contribution towards the push to federalism, he "will be seen as the Dean of Canada's modern provincial rights movement."[193] More than the other things he did combined, this will have the major long term effect on Canada, because a true federal state is needed for Canada to survive. The old way of doing things within a confederated government structure is archaic and is too rigid. Its rigid nature strains the bonds of nationalism. There will be more Indian brockades and oil wars and referendums, each chipping away at, if not breaking, one of the world's most respected countries.

The patriation of the British North America Act (BNA) is the single most important political event in modern Canadian history. It gives Canadians the tool to save their country, threatened by simmering resentment underlined by the Quebec separation referendum loss by only 0.58% and ambitious regions that are confident in their ability to do better than the central government.

Although patriation of the BNA ended the last vestige[194] of English colonialism in CANADA, it did not decisively and conclusively make CANADA a country. Quebec, the driving reason for patriation in the first place, refused to sign on. Without Quebec's participation, Canada's future is vulnerable. Eventually, this vulnerability, left unresolved, will be the end of CANADA.

---

employment experience President Harry Truman had, but he authorized dropping the atomic bombs on Japan.

[193] ipolitics, Dr Michael Behiels, Professor of Constitutional History, Peter Lougheed, dean of Canada's modern provincial rights movement, September 21, 2012. [Provincial rights are an echo of states' rights, a clarion call in many American jurisprudence disputes.]

[194] Actually, the Constitution document is a remnant of colonialism as it was written by the English, as opposed to the American constitution, which was written to meet the needs of, for, and by the people of the new country when it separated from Britain.

Without oil, there would not have been a Peter Lougheed. Money is power, and oil gave him power to play a leading role in the constitution fight. His fight, in the final analysis, was therefore for money.

Pierre Trudeau, on the other hand, did not need oil. He fought for a cause — the future of CANADA. He knew the country needed a tool to fix its unforgiving rigid structure, and that tool was a constitution it could control. His vison and courage gave CANADA a heart and soul by adding *The Charter of Rights and Freedoms* to an otherwise plain administrative constitution, which in the long term will make him Canada's most inspiring leader.

The two forms of government are mutually exclusive. One has direction from the centre out; the other has direction from out to the centre. Neither however, has independent long-term life without nationhood.

It is often said that Canada became a nation when its soldiers captured Vimy Ridge in World War I, a victory several armies from other countries failed to achieve. Mike Mountain Horse was there. He was fighting there. Over the four days of the battle, there were over 10,000[195] Canadian casualties beside him. It was the shared spirit of Mike and his comrades that gave us a sense of nationhood ..... something that no form of government could or will ever do.

23 Vimy Memorial

Domestic and or geo-political events will eventually move CANADA from a confederation to a federation. With determined political leadership this movement could be a more controlled change, determined because it would take a constitutional change. The constitutional change is a transfer of the central government's residual rights to the provinces, a change that the provinces could initiate. They could initiate and

---

[195] COOK TIM, *Vimy the Battle and The Legend*, 2018.

control this with the constitution's amending formula that gives them the potential numbers required for amending it.

The residual rights, or powers, are currently assigned to the Federal Government[196]. The language for this assignment could be swapped with the language of Section 92 which would give the Federal Government the power to make laws *exclusively only regarding the powers stated for the Federal Government in Section 91*; while giving the provinces the power to make legislation pursuant to Section 92 as well as those not listed in Section 91.

Such a change would give CANADA the Lougheed federal structure. But in my opinion, this will never happen because it takes away Ontario's authority as a colonizer, which Ontario will never allow to happen.

What do we need to do to get what we want for our future, which is not as difficult to do as it is to agree on what we want, and who gets it and how much.

In the beginning all this was decided for us. ENGLAND created CANADA and CANADA created *Alberta* and *Alberta* created Calgary, which in the early history of this country worked out pretty good for those sparsely settled areas with people living in this cornucopia of plenty enjoying one of the highest standards of living ever on earth, as the country was mostly overlooked fortunately, by the vicissitudes of international history.

The constitution tool, although in its first line appears to leave responsibility for what happens to us, to "the supremacy of God", whoever that might be, there is some room for us to be accountable to ourselves. The Constitution Act, 1867 Section V. Provincial Constitutions recognizes the constitutions for Ontario, Quebec, Nova Scotia, and New Brunswick. This is analogous to the original Canadian Constitution giving these four provinces ownership of natural resources but not the same ownership for *Alberta*. *Alberta* made sure that was changed. It is time for *Alberta* to introduce a provincial constitution.

---

[196] Section 91, Powers of the Parliament. {…. all Matters not assigned exclusively to the Legislatures …]

But be careful. Mention the word constitution at a party and you will be amazed how quickly you are standing alone. Use the words job description for politicians and you will be the centre of the party. Although a constitution is the most crucial authority for everything in a country, as opposed to the army as it is in some countries, it is not the most easily explained and communicated thing to the majority of voters who all have their own job descriptions, which many view as prison sentences and would be surprised to learn that *Alberta* politicians, and consequently civic politicians as well, do not have a job description.

So, the *Alberta* and municipal governments need job descriptions, notwithstanding *The Municipal Government Act*. The *Alberta* Government needs a job description (constitution) to put it on an equal footing with the other provinces in Canada's inexorable evolution from a confederation to federation.

Civic governments need a job description to give those governed some control over those they elect. For example, the current "job description" gives the councils the authority to spend on things that are in "the opinion of council … desirable", like $6 billion Olympic Games and $600 million hockey rinks while cutting police and fire services. Calgary Council needs to be reformed, and it needs a job description that includes citizen-initiated, enforceable referendums.

Freedom from The Indian Act

If Mike Mountain Horse had been white, he would have been an officer and decorated for bravery. He served three years in the Canadian Army during World War I, rising from the lowest rank to Acting Sergeant, an obvious indication that the Army recognized his leadership ability.

As a leader, he led soldiers behind enemy lines and captured a machine gun nest. On another occasion he captured several enemy and shot a resisting officer while doing so. He also used his knife in an encounter to kill two others. An exploding shell covered him for several days before he was discovered.

The City of Lethbridge, where he resided and worked after the War, recognized his community citizenship by naming a school after him.

Mike Mountain Horse overcame *The Indian Act* that imprisons reserve Indians and keeps them from benefiting from Canadian citizenship. It is not money that will free these Indians, it is abolishing *The Indian Act* that will; and, since Canada's Parliament created the Act, only the Parliament can abolish the Act. It is past time for Canadians to set Indians free.

Politically passive province punching above its weight

If there was not oil, there would not have a Peter Lougheed. Oil gave an otherwise politically passive province the capacity to punch above its weight during an uncertain time when the old, centralized version of Canada was being threatened by a new decentralized vision of the country.

If Quebec had not actually taken the first step to separate and Prime Minister Joe Clark had properly counted the votes needed in Parliament to withstand a non-confidence vote, Pierre Trudeau would not have been resurrected from the politically dead to create a *Charter of Rights and Freedoms* in what was essentially an administrative document known as the *British North America Act*.

The *Charter of Rights and Freedoms* will, over time, give CANADA a heart and soul and give it a foundation, transforming it from a country to a nation.

Premier Peter Lougheed and Prime Minister Pierre Trudeau were leaders, although opposite and opposing types. Lougheed was a self-assured, straight ahead management type who leveraged *Alberta*'s strategic grip on oil supply to push the Constitution in the direction of a new decentralized Canada. TRUDEAU was a determined dreamer who strove to preserve his poetic vision of the old CANADA, which included grabbing as much (i.e. *Alberta*'s oil wealth) as the central government could from its western Canadian colonies.

And Mike Mountain Horse, a hero, fought in blood and body parts at Vimy Ridge, beside 10,000[197] Canadian casualties, so each political leader could have the freedom to pursue his vision.

---

[197] The Canadian attack was the first time all four Canadian divisions had fought together. Their success was due to thorough planning, lengthy training, and tactical innovations.

By the end of the War, 60,000 Canadians had been killed, equivalent to a quarter of a million in today's figures. As well as Vimy, Mike survived major battles at Hill 70, Cambrai, and Amiens.

Mike Mountain Horse's heritage can be seen in the breeze through trackless prairie grass; in unbridled horses pasturing in a meadow; in the forested foothills before the Rocky Mountains; in the scree of a hunting hawk — all reigned over by Chief Mountain, the mountain that looked down on him every morning of his youth ..... and the mountain that he now looks up at every day from his grave.

The Lougheeds and the Trudeaus come and go, but Mike Mountain Horse's timeless spirit will be in the land forever.

"The future ain't what it used to be"[198]

If making love in a canoe[199] makes you Canadian, then floating your boat in a late summer wheat field makes you an *Alberta*n.

Alberta was wheat fields long before oil, and will be long after[200]. In the long-term history of civilization, oil, because it cannot be re-planted every Spring like wheat, was destined to be a short fling. However, it was one hell of a ride for *Alberta*ns.

You cannot argue with the future. You can argue about it, but you cannot argue with it. The only thing that can be said with certainty about the future is that it will be different than today. As a famous Greek philosopher said "the only thing constant in life is change"[201].

What is the future? Is it Charlton Heston's (actor and political activist) trilogy *Planet of the Apes (1968)*, where nuclear Armageddon relegates humans to a disappearing trace of its once dominant place at the top of the food chain; *Omega Man (1971)*, where a world-wide plague has left the few survivors fighting each other to live; or *Soylent*

---

[198] TIME MAGAZINE, *Yogi Berra: Baseball legend, accidental philosopher*, October 5, 2015.

[199] Attributed to Pierre Berton, famous Canadian author from the Yukon, who denied it but accepted it because it was as good as any other definition of a Canadian,: "A Canadian is someone who knows how to make love in a canoe", 1973.

[200] Food and shelter are the two imperative needs of humans, and always will be. Oil just enables people to produce more of them and for more people.

[201] At a party, I dropped this little truism and attributed it to Hercules. A philosophy scholar in the group quickly and very dryly pointed out that Hercules was he of much brawn, and that it was Heraclitus who said change is the only constant in life. Which just goes to show you, what do I know.

A theoretical embellishment around this truism emanates from the basis of the American film titled Back to the Future staring Canadian Michael J. Fox. This film, populist and successful as it may have been, probably settled the debate more decisively and conclusively than any congregation of Greek philosophers sitting around the campfire drinking wine, or whatever those guys drank in those days.

Green (1973), where environmental indifference has reduced humans to processing dead bodies and eating them in order to survive.

A current Danish streaming series, *The Rain (2018),* deals with a quest by young people who seem to have morals, so lacking in the pandemic-stricken adults hunting them, guiding their decisions to find a vaccine for a hundred per cent certain "to-kill-you-in-seconds" virus.

The origin of the phrase *"When in danger or in doubt, run in circles scream and shout"* is uncertain. Most references cite a military origin, likely around the Second World War. However, one authority quotes a remote Mongolian General as the origin.[202]

Mongolians are often thought of as being rather impolite in the manner in which they slaughtered their way to the world's largest ever empire (the English and the Spanish were of course much more considerate as they acquired their empires).

Modern historians note the other more democratic side of the Mongol image after the conquests. Mongols were generally considered reasonable in allowing local governance and implementing tax regimes conducive to trade rather than regulated robbery. This resulted in the exchange of culture and philosophy. Inherent in this broad intermixing, religious toleration[203] was officially enforced and supported

In a bizarre way, the Mongols had an early trace of what we now call democracy, which is intended to tolerate the public presence, providing it does not unduly interfere or interrupt government. When it does interfere and government loses its elasticity, that's when people run in circles scream and shout. Which is where North American democracy is today.

Screaming and shouting has always been a characteristic of society, in various degrees and loudness. Now, with easily accessible

---

[202] Since there is no consensus on the origin of the phrase "When in danger ...", I am sticking with Herman Wouk, The Caine Mutiny, 1951, all of whose books I have read. One even has a major character named after me (..... a little dry Indian humour).

[203] Peter, Frankopan, The Silk Roads: A New History of the World, 2018.

electronic communication, there seems to be much more screaming and shouting than ever. Anyone with access to a cell phone or a computer feels compelled to broadcast an opinion about everything, regardless of what they know, and more often, what they do not know.

The scope and grasp of digital data gathering, analyzing, and distributing information widens the gap, either real or imagined, actual or perceived, between those who govern and those who are governed, diminishing the trust between the two that is the essence needed to ensure a democratic society works. A new definition of democracy is needed to save democracy.

No beer sold to Indians

He could not buy a beer.

After fighting for CANADA at Vimy Ridge, Cambrai, Amiens, and Hill 70, and being wounded four times, once buried for four days behind enemy lines while a German soldier ate his lunch while sitting on the debris that covered him, Mike came home to Southern *Alberta* where he could not buy a beer.

Because he was an Indian!

But my father, a white man and non-combatant army cook, could. So Mike and his Indian friends would wait in their pickup in our back yard while my father went to buy them beer. And wine. Cheap wine by the gallon.

In his later years, Mike recognized the harm of this bootlegging and the damage it did to his people,[204] as he lamented in his book, white men "providing the Indians with 'firewater', which always resulted in brawls and killings".

There was, and still is, a fence —*The Indian Act*, a product of Canada's Parliament. It keeps Canadians and Indians apart, denying each the opportunity to learn from and to share each others' culture. Naming a road or a building after an Indian does not do it.

There was, and still is, a fence —*The Indian Act*, a product of Canada's Parliament. It keeps Canadians and Indians apart, denying each the opportunity to learn from and to share each others' culture. Naming a road or a building after an Indian does not do It is time to set Indians free, —abolish the Indian Act.

---

[204] Adam Beach, a modern successful Canadian Indian actor reflects this same recognition in the movie titled Ice Soldiers (2013) wherein he says he can not go into a bar because of the "demons inside". Look closely at his eyes and you can see he is doing more than merely presenting a line in a movie script.

Success in two cultures

A hero is an ordinary person overcoming extraordinary circumstances which inspires and leads others.

In my opinion.

We see heroes "differently, depending". There are many different opinions, all with merit or value, which when compared to other opinions give each more depth, more meaning.

Mike Mountain Horse was a hero because he successfully lived in two conflicting cultures, one immensely more dominant than the other. The first culture was his Indian world that was struggling to hang onto the old ways of doing things while denying the world had moved on — he recognized this. The second culture was the relentless non-Indian world of mass societies that inexorably rolled on, Indian resistance notwithstanding.

His Indian culture recognized Mike's inspiration and honoured him by electing him a minor chief, a leader.

Mike's non-Indian culture recognized his contribution and awarded him with three military stripes and a medal for his gallantry in World War I; and, after a lifetime of community service in Lethbridge, named a school after him.

Succeeding simultaneously in two conflicting cultures, Mike Mountain Horse was a trailblazer for today's Indian.

Indigenous: endangered species, extinct species

How Indigenous leaders describe their society as having less education, less health care, less housing; etcetera than other Canadians gives the impression that it is an endangered species.

Unfortunately, the leaders blame this condition on non-Indians. It is historically true that Indians suffered from the immigration of European hordes and their cultures, but current Indigenous societies must take some responsibility for their success or failure. Or the next phase of endangered is extinct species.

Extinction can be avoided. An independent and self-assured Mike Mountain Horse did it. Others can too, if we leave them alone.

The endangered species

	Indigenous	Non-Indigenous
Employment	57 %	62%
Medium income	$21,253	$31,144
Post secondary education	68 %	70 %
Decaying housing	20 %	6 %
First Nation over-crowding	37 % on reserves	19 % off reserves
Life expectancy	10 -15 years shorter	
Infant mortality	2 – 4 times higher	
Suicide rates	6 times higher for youth	
Food insecurity	48 %	8 %
Prison	20 %	

Children living with grandparents	21 %	10 %
Children in foster care	~50% of all children in Canada	

Source: SAWCHUK, JOE, *Social conditions of Indigenous Peoples in Canada,* The Canadian Encyclopedia, October w1, 2011.

"The Indian Problem"

Throwing money at it has not solved the "Indian Problem". Nor will it.

The *Truth & Reconciliation* program of the Canadian Government will not change the pattern of past public prejudice.

It is difficult to determine the origin of the phrase "The Indian Problem". It can be seen in the speeches of the successful American civil war general and eventual president of THE UNITED STATES Ulysses Grant. Subsequent president Theodore Roosevelt (1901) uttered it in countless campaign stumps.

Did CANADA get the phrase, like so many other things Canadian, by association with the U.S. Probably not. Canada's first legislation, *The Indian Act,* by its mere existence is directed towards solving the Indian Problem. The *Act* cites the need to end the dependence of Indians upon the Government and prepare them for survival from the inevitable wave of modernity.

Canada has its own prejudices, for example "none is too many[205]" is a phrase used in the Government of Prime Minister Mackenzie King when considering how many Jews would be allowed to immigrate into Canada during and after[206] the *Second World War*. Or the Canadian *internment* camps for Canadian-Ukrainians during the *First World* or the *internment* of Japanese-Canadians during the *Second*.

But whatever the reason for these discriminations against Canadians, there does not linger the Jewish problem, or the Ukrainian problem, or the Japanese problem. This can be debated forever, but the fact remains there is still the Indian Problem, otherwise why is there a need for today's *Truth and Reconciliation*?

The popular word today for Canada's historical treatment of the Indians is "genocide". There was no genocide in CANADA. There was genocide in EUROPE when 6,000,000 Jews were murdered; there was genocide in RWANDA when 200,000 were murdered (1994, when the myth of CANADA as a "peacekeeper" was shattered). This was genocide.

---

[205] Troper, Harold, and Irving Abella, *None is too many:* Key Porter Books, 1993,

[206] After more than 6,000,000 million Jews had just been murdered in Europe.

Whatever happened to Canadian Indians was not genocide. To say it was hides from view what happened. Most will not believe that thousands of Indians were murdered in residential schools; or that those murdered were buried in mass graves as exclaimed by Indian leaders who used the words murdered or killed to describe what happened.

Many unmarked graves have been recently discovered, but that does not mean they were mass graves. Mass graves are those with many people in one, as though a backhoe was used to dig them and bulldozers pushed bodies in. These things did not happen. Most graves are unmarked because wooden markers were used and they rotted and fell down over almost a century. Even many more solid markers in non-Indian cemeteries decayed over that time – just visit the older part of any cemetery.

Tell it like it really was otherwise the stories lose credibility, and also support for any public accountability like *Truth & Reconciliation*. Residential schools at the time were considered reasonable attempts to solve the Indian Problem. Apparently, it did not. Indian leaders without hesitation complain about higher infant mortality, lower levels of education achievement, lower health care, unsafe water supplies, high unemployment, etcetera.

Statistics show these to be credible when they are compared to statistics of the country's population. However, it is also interesting to compare the statistics of Indigenous people living on reserves to those not living off reserves.[207] From the graphic below, it appears to be better to be Indigenous off reserve – depending on whether or not one's point of view is the old ways of living or the modern.

But why? What type of Indigenous person left the reserve and why?

---

[207] Which leads to the next section "The Indian Industry".

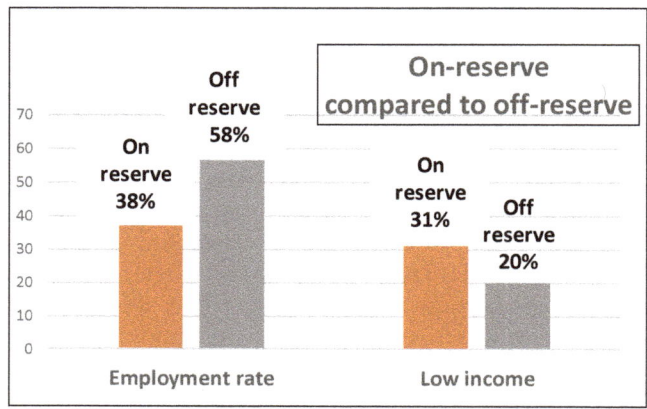

24 On-reserve compared to off-reserve

Guardian newspaper
Statistics Canada, Census of population 2021

So, what is The Indian Problem? There are many ways to define it, but it is helpful too look at it from two points of view: at the beginning of the last century and currently.

Is there a difference between the two. The first might be characterized as a time when many Indians were anticipating a time the white man would disappear from the continent"[208]. They resisted change while living it. For example, in 1968 Chief Johnny Smallboy of the Erminskine Band on the Hobbema Reserve in central *Alberta* led 125 tribal members to the western foothills of the Rocky Mountains where they set up tents. His stated purpose was "to return to the land". Camp members were asked to:

> *give up the trappings of modern society, including*
> *television, drugs, and alcohol; follow the Indian*

---

[208] Ibid, Mike Mountain Horse.

> *Way, adopting traditional rituals and traditional*
> *Indian medicine.[209]*

With the onset of the first winter, trucks from the camp went into the nearest town (Nordegg) for propane space heaters for the tents. The camp lasted about two years when it split into two factions. Many of the followers returned to the Hobbema Reserve where:

> *They were not deprived of their share of the oil roy-*
> *alties that occurred in 1970's & 1980's and gave*
> *each member of Ermineskin Band, man, woman, &*
> *child five hundred dollars a month. Smallboy had*
> *initially taken his band to the foothills to help alle-*
> *viate poverty, however the Ermineskin band soon*
> *became the richest band in the land[210]*

It is difficult not to conclude that The Indian Problem is Indians wanting it both ways - to live the old ways while living the modern way.

The old ways are gone while the modern way is an undeniable force, for non-Indians as well as Indians. Indians want their children educated in their native language. Fine. Tell that to an Indigenous teenager using her Indian language while trying to order a slurpy at the local *Seven-Elven.*

---

[209] BOTTING, GARY, *The Pursuit of Freedom*, Fifth House Books, 2005. The quote is from Amazon books online.

The Ineffectiveness of "Traditional Indian Medicine" was revealed during the Covid Pandemic of 2020. In an effort to contain the epidemic, the Canadian Government limited large gatherings. Indians refused, asserting they were a sovereign nation and therefore did not have to comply. To demonstrate this, they held a Sun Dance. Then, when a vaccine for the virus was discovered, they claimed they should be the first to get it. It was hard for many non-Indians to understand the logic behind this.

[210] Robert Smallboy - Wikipedia

"The Indian Industry"

Sucking dollars ...

"Indian industry — an army of consultants, lawyers and accountants who are sucking hundreds of millions of dollars out of First Nations and from federal government coffers." [211]

Add to this list entrepreneurs both big and small who include an Indian component. Governments have check lists when assessing projects for funding and grants. The checklists have boxes for things like region, employment potential, etcetera, and then boxes for Indigenous and for Metis, the latter which may have nothing to do with proposals but have more weight than the other boxes.

For example, the federal Government is trying to finagle the sale of *Trans Mountain Pipeline* to the Indians. The Government bought the pipeline from a private company for about $4.5 billion. Then it spent about $30.9 billion [212]to twin the line. Total government investment equals at least $35 billion.

About 75 Indigenous groups contiguous to the pipeline think it would be a good idea to own the pipeline and are negotiating the possibility. Ownership, says *Project Reconciliation*, one of two Indigenous groups vying to buy the pipeline, would "bring funding for critical infrastructure like housing, roads, sewers and drinking water". [213]

Now. A simple question. Indigenous people continuously exclaim extreme poverty — WHERE ARE THEY GOING TO GET MONEY FOR THE PURCHASE OF A $35 BILLION PIPELINE?

The answer: FROM CANADIAN TAXPAYERS WHO OWN THE LINE!

The federal government has a divestment process whereby it hopes to return *Trans Mountain* to the private sector. It is unlikely a private bidder would win the bid for the pipeline even offering twice

---

[211] POPPLEWELL, BRETT, *An Indian Industry has emerged amid the wreckage of many Candain reserves*, Toronto Star, October 30 2010.

[212] VARCOE, CHRIS, *Alberta's premier concerned about potential two year delay of Trans Mountain expansion*, Calgary Herald, December 22, 2023.

[213] BAKX, KYLE, *Plans to sell Trans Mountain pipeline to Indigenous groups take another step forward*, CBC, February 2021.

The other potential Indigenous "buyer" is named Western Indigenous Pipeline Group.

what any Indigenous group would offer. However, this scenario would be unlikely because private bidders would not even bother bidding knowing the cards were stacked against them.

The check boxes are very prominent in applications for the theatre. In fact, dispensers of government funds require a certain level of Indigenous participation for anything they do. For example, the CBC. The public broadcaster has an annual budget of $1.4 billion, which is about $50 per Canadian taxpayer per year. Of this money, 30% must go to "Diversity, Equity, and Inclusion"; that is a code words for Indigenous.[214]

---

[214] National Post, *Diversity quotas put on CBC spending*, August 2022. www.wordpress.com

Solving the Indian problem

They claim to be sovereign. Sovereignty generally means having control over everything within a recognised geographical area. Therefore, for more than a hundred years reservations refused to reveal to the federal government what had been done with the annual money given them, for whatever program or reason. That is, no accountability like any other recipient across Canada: provinces, cities large and small, organizations, etcetera. It is even difficult for Statistics CANADA to get cooperation for the Census because the reserves say it is none of Canada's business.

When the Canadian Government, to contain the Covid pandemic sought to regulate gatherings, a Saskatchewan tribe said no, we are sovereign; and to demonstrate held a Sun Dance. But when a vaccine for Covid was found, the same Indians said to the Federal Government that they should be the first to receive it because they were Indigenous. Defying the government and then seeking its aid is bizarre. Either you are sovereign, or you aren't.

Sovereignty is more than just control: it is responsibility for those within the sovereign area. For this reason the Canadian Government has exercised control over reservations ensuring a standard of living comparable to other parts of CANADA. Indigenous people have accepted this generosity as an obligation of the Canadian Government. They rationalize this as a fiduciary right. A fiduciary right is broad but generally exists between parties where one is entrusted to act for the best interest of another. This is a trust relationship that is ethical, or moral or legal. I do not think there is any specific legislation that spells out a legal fiduciary obligation between Indigenous people living on the reservation and the Canadian Government. However, it may be deduced that there is because of *The Indian Act*.

The Indian Act divides and separates Indians and non-Indians. It perpetuates "them versus us" preventing Indigenous people from participating in and enjoying the benefits of modern society. The *Act* must go to end the Indian problem.

Abolishing the *Act* raises the question of what to do with the land on which Reserves are situated. The land does not belong to its residents; it belongs to the Crown (that is, the Government) which only set it aside for use of the tribes. Title of the land was retained by the Crown.

Title to the land used by the Tribes should go to the Tribes. Then the Tribes can decide what to do with it. For example, an Indigenous person could apply for a mortgage to build a home.

The overall result of abolishing *The Indian Act* would be that Tribes and their members would have ultimate responsibility for their own success of failure.

This can be construed as sovereignty which means full self control; it also means self financing.

Truth & Reconciliation - One hand clapping:

"Truth & Reconciliation" too often sounds like one hand clapping. That is:

- One hand truth - repeating recognized history, but
- One hand reconciliation - saying little.

Truth and reconciliation began in South Africa as an apology for Apartheid. Apartheid was the legal separation of the black majority from the white minority that held legislative authority that had been established through colonization.

Black families numbering several millions[215] were taken from their homes and forced to live in government designated areas. This institutionalized segregation lasted from 1948 to 1993, although it was condemned by the UNITED NATIONS and received a 25-year trade embargo from CANADA.

In CANADA, truth and reconciliation is the result of class actions taken against the Government of Canada that funded and the churches that operated Indian Residential Schools. The Government of Canada settled out of court. The settlement is known as the *Indian Residential Schools Settlement Agreement (2005).*

What is now quietly referred to by bureaucrats among themselves as the "Indian Problem" began with the beginning of CANADA confederation. In 1876 the *Indian Act* was passed. Although the *Act* has been amended since then, the changes have been mostly for administrative convenience rather than intent. That intent is, after more than one and a half centuries later, open to interpretation, but its age certainly leaves itself open to the question of how it can still be relevant in today's modern world. A couple of voices from the time of the Act gives some idea of its intent:

> *"our Indian legislation ... to aid the Red man in lifting himself out of his condition of tutelage and dependence ... to prepare him for a higher civilization by encouraging him to assume the privileges and responsibilities of full citizenship"[216]*

---

[215] Compared to about 150,000 Indians placed in Canadian residential schools.

[216] Department of the Interior, Government of Canada.

furthermore

"the great aim of our legislation has been to do away with the tribal system and assimilate the In-ian people in all respects [217]

It is always difficult to understand previous generation's intentions through prisms using modern standards. The best that can be said about *The Indian Act* is that the most informed minds at the time felt that first, there was a need to do something; and second, *The Indian Act* was al that good be done. That is, in the1800s the *Act's* promoters were sincere and well intentioned, given prevailing attitudes.

However, since after more than a century there still is a feeling that something must be done, which was the reason for *Truth & Reconciliation*. It is also proof that the *Act* failed to be that "something" needed and that it had unintended consequences.

The quote from the Department of the Interior and the Prime Minister are fairly clear:

Reference	Goal	Result
Department of the Interior	End Indian dependence on the Government	Continuous and increasing funding of Reserves is evidence of failure
Prime Minister Macdonald	a) Eliminate the Tribal system b) Assimilate the Indians	a) Indigenous claims of sovereignty shows Tribal system still exists b) Reserve Indians not assimilated

---

[217] Hughes, Aaron, 10 Days That Shaped Modern Canada, University of Albert Press, 2022.

Indigenous People	More Government funding	Dissatisfaction and discontent
Assembly of First Nations	Entrenchment of the right of self government in the Canadian Constitution	Partial success by Section 25 of The Charter of Rights and Freedom
The Canadian public	Domestic harmony	Annoyed with un-ending Indigenous demands and civil disorder

In practical terms, the reality is that abstract concepts and "government down" programs did not exorcise the Indian problem. Throwing money at the problem, as the Government has done for decades, does not work. It only fuels demand for more money. When the last dollar of the $5 billion for *Truth & Reconciliation* is spent, living conditions on the reserves will not be better and the public perception of Reserve Indians will not be any different. If the goal of *Truth & Reconciliation* is to improve self image, that must come from Indigenous themselves.

Social engineering, for Indigenous or non-Indigenous, by governments is seldom successful. Change comes from those within society. For change to happen, Indians must paddle their own canoe. (please see page 21).

Mike Mountain Horse distinguished himself as a soldier serving three years in the terrible trenches of World War I. He ended his military service as an acting sergeant.

He was elected a minor Chief of his tribe and also a president of a non-Indigenous railway labour union.

He earned a railway pension from working off-reserve. He was a well-known public speaker, including regular story telling to non-Indigenous children at the public library.

Mike Mountain Horse was "one of the most popular figures in Lethbridge".

Mike did not need *Truth & Reconciliation*, nor any other government program. Neither does any young proud Indian today. .

———————————————————————————————

"Queues of Indians" on English P.M.'s doorstep

The threat of Quebec separation has always hung over CANADA. It has been used by Quebec to derive more from the Canadian Government; that is, the rest of CANADA (RoC).

Indeed, the precedent was set at the time of confederation in 1867. As a condition of joining CANADA, Quebec was guaranteed a specified number of senate and judicial seats. Quebec law is based on the Napoleonic Code while the rest of Canadian law is based on English common law, more formally referred to as stare decisis[218]. In recent years, it is often publicly alleged that Quebec puts less into CANADA while continuously taking more out.

The need for this different treatment, it is argued by Quebec, is because Quebec is a "distinct society". Many in Quebec interpret this distinctness as a justification for separation from CANADA, as manifested politically in the *Quebec Sovereignty Act.*[219] *Quebec has held two referendums calling for separation, the most* recent in 1990 in which separation lost by only a near death margin of less than one percent.

Prime Minister, Pierre Trudeau, in the decade leading up to this vote had become frustrated with the inability of his political colleagues to deal with Quebec's discontent with CANADA. The expression of that discontent had grown from simply painting mailboxes to small bombs to kidnapping a senior British diplomat to murdering a deputy premier of the Quebec Government.

Prime Minister Pierre Trudeau concluded that the only way CANADA could deal with the national distress created by Quebec's open discontent was to change the basic fabric of the country. This was the same conclusion of numerous federal and provincial leaders for over half a century. They realized the only way to change that fabric was by a change in the Canadian Constitution. However, numerous constitution conferences had all failed.

Beside disagreement over what kind of changes should be made, the constitution conferences ultimately failed because Canada did not

---

[218]"The legal principle of determining points in litigation according to precedent".

[219] *The Alberta Sovereignty Act* is inherently not much different since its long-term affect will be "ten little Countries".

have a constitution — it had an <u>act</u> of the British Parliament that defined the country and the authorities of the governments. Therefore, since it was a British Act, the Canadian Government could not change it, only the British could.

The Canadian Government did not have control of its own destiny. Pierre Trudeau determined to change that! And to change it with or without unanimous agreement from the provinces, which he believed would never happen.

Prime Miniter Pierre Trudeau made it his mission to save CANADA, and that could be done only by getting a constitution into Canadian's hands so that they could save themselves. His means of doing that was to convince the British Government to legislatively hand down to CANADA the *British North America Act* of 1867 (BNA), since that was the de facto constitution of CANADA.

Well, that provoked Canadian politicians from "A Mari Usque Ad Mare" to "run in circles, scream and shout".

No province supported the Prime Minister's initiative because they felt another province would get something that it did not. So the Prime Minister essentially said to hell with provincial premiers and lobbied the British Government, convincing them that the BNA was an archaic residual from colonial days.

Trudeau was not the only one that lobbied the British Government. Eight provincial premiers, led by Alberta Premier Lougheed, started a public relations campaign in CANADA and ENGLAND against what became known as the patriation of the constitution.

It was not only politicians that lobbied for and against patriation. There were 294 different groups, several of which were Indigenous. The Indigenous groups were against patriation because they worried that the special connection between them and the English crown would be broken, thus leaving them subject to the whims of the new ultimate constitutional authority the Canadian Government.

The Indigenous lobbying was noticed. A "delegation of aboriginal chiefs and elders had spent a week in London, seeking British help". The

British Prime Minister said that "she had no desire to deal with 'queues of Indians'" knocking on her 10 Downing Street door to voice objections about Canada's plan to patriate the Constitution."[220] At the time Trudeau was facing increasing public opposition to his plan that had a charter of rights and freedoms, the heart and soul of any constitution. Feeling a need to move things along, he compromised. He agreed to a clause that essentially excepted Indigenous people from the new Canadian Constitution:

> *General 25. The guarantee in this Charter of certain rights and freedoms shall not be construed so as to abrogate or derogate from any aboriginal, treaty or other rights or freedoms that pertain to the aboriginal peoples of Canada including (a) any rights or freedoms that have been recognized by the Royal Proclamation of October 7, 1763; and (b) any rights or freedoms that now exist by way of land claims agreements or may be so acquired[221]*

Essentially, this means CANADA has two constitutions: one for Indigenous people and one for other Canadians.

Prime Minister Pierre Trudeau made another compromise that has implications for Indigenous People. This compromise is known as the "notwithstanding clause" that gives any province that so wishes to except itself from the *Charter*. This clause was introduced and championed by Premier Lougheed of Alberta[222]..

> *33.(1) Parliament or the legislature of a province may expressly declare in an Act of Parliament or of the legislature, as the case may be, that the Act or a provision thereof shall operate*

---

[220] THE CANADIAN PRESS, August 2, 2012.

[221] Canadian Charter of Rights and Freedoms, *Constitution of Canada 1982*.

[222] The purpose of the notwithstanding clause was to give wiggle room to legislatures when basic rights were inconvenient for Government legislation. When the clause was introduced, there was much concern expressed by lawyers and human rights activists. They maintained that human rights were human rights regardless of political convenience.

notwithstanding a provision included in section 2 or sections 7 to 15 of this Charter. (2) An Act or a provision of an Act in respect of which a declaration made under this section is in effect shall have such operation as it would have but for the provision of this Charter referred to in the declaration. (3) A declaration made under subsection (1) shall cease to have effect five years after it comes into force or on such earlier date as may be specified in the declaration. (4) Parliament or the legislature of a province may re-enact a declaration made under subsection (1). (5) Subsection (3) applies in respect of a re-enactment made under subsection (4).[223]

Since the patriation of the constitution, Quebec has used this notwithstanding clause to declare every federal legislation to be void in Quebec.

The implication for Indigenous People is that legislation can vary across provinces, depending on which province invokes the notwithstanding clause and for what purpose.

Canada therefore has a patchwork, or checkerboard, idea of what are rights and freedoms.

―――――――――――――――

Indigenous people more often than not saw their agreements or treaties as between themselves and the British monarchy — between them and the great white father or mother — and not the Canadian Government. They saw the monarch as the protector of their rights. So their reaction to Trudeau's initiative was negative because they likened it to cutting their umbilical cord and subjecting them to the vagaries of the Canadian public.

―――――――――――――――

[223] Mr Lougheed, the Alberta premier who successfully championed the notwithstanding clause for both the *Alberta Bill of Rights* and *The Canadian Charter of Rights and Freedoms*, claimed he knew nothing about a notwithstanding clause until his Attorney General said *"Premier, we will have to provide in this Bill* [that is, the *Alberta Bill of Rights*] *for a notwithstanding clause"*. (University Of Calgary, November 20, 1991)

The result of the de facto Indigenous constitution is separation; the result of the notwithstanding clause may be different rights for Indigenous people in different provinces.

Separation and differentiation is what CANADA has now. Indigenous people are separated from the rest of CANADA by *The Indian Act*; many of them are, for all practicable purposes, fenced[224] off on reserves. The section in the Canadian Constitution that exempt Indigenous people is differentiation. The notwithstanding clause in the Constitution can result in different laws for Indigenous in different provinces.

The bottom line of what Indigenous people may see as protecting them is nothing more than protecting the status quo, which, as evidenced by the need for *Truth & Reconciliation* is not working. They perpetuate separation.

The week before Mike Mountain Horse died, he was in the Indian Hospital. Across the street from this hospital was the non-Indian hospital! Why? Why was there a need for side-by-side hospitals – one for Indians and one for non-Indians.

Another example of institutionalized discrimination. Canada has a National Day of Remembrance on November 11 honouring veterans. But not for Indian veterans. They have their own remembrance day.

These different treatments of Indigenous people is just modern separation and discrimination. They perpetuate the separateness of cultures.

A separate remembrance day for non-Indians; whose idea was that? If it was the idea of non-Indians, is that discrimination or polite paternalism. If the idea was Indian, are they discriminating. Who ever had the idea had a dumb idea. It separates Canadians.

The inevitable result of separation is difference; in the case of Indigenous versus non-Indigenous it is a different standard of living. As Indigenous leaders continuously point out, it is a lower standard of living for reserve people. If Indian leaders want to raise the stand of living of reserve people, do not perpetuate the separation that is inherent in *The Indian Act*. Abolish the *Act*. Then Indigenous people with have full Canadian citizenship along with the full benefits of Canadian society.

---

[224] For example, it is difficult for a non-Indian to visit a reserve without being harassed.

"The Indian Problem"; "The Indian Industry"; "The dirty Old Indian".

If we can not say these words because they may offend, they and their undertone will not go away.

If we can not say these words because they may offend, how will we know what we want to go away?

If we can not say these words because they may offend, how can we say which way to go?

The author is not an Indian

I always thought, and still do, that Mike was my grandfather.

But his army enlistment paper[225] has the following questions and answers:

Attestation questions	Mike's answers
What is the name of your next of kin?	Mary Mountain Horse
What is the relationship of your next of kin?	Wife
Are you married?	Yes

When beginning this manuscript, that to me was decisive and conclusive. I knew Mike and I knew my grandmother Mary Mountain Horse (nee Potaina). The Attestation Paper said they were married at the time Mike enlisted and, in my experience, still were after the Second World War.

However, the name of the father on my mother's birth certificate was not Mountain Horse. This was a mystery. I rationalized this by concluding that Mike and Mary had separated for a time between the Wars. But I was not comfortable with this. I decided to go more deeply into his military records which were about three centimetres thick, and handwritten, and, because they were old and faded were very difficult to understand.

Halfway through the pile was a document titled *Particulars of an Officer or Man Enlisted in C.E.F.*, dated February 15, 1917. The main purpose of this document seemed to be Mike's assignment of his Separation Pay[226] to:

Mary AGNES Mountain Horse.

---

[225] Attestation Paper #895041, May 23, 1916.

[226] In this document Mike gives his place of birth as Brocket on the Peigan Reserve whereas in his Attestation Papers he says he was born on the Blood Reserve.

However, my grandmother's name was Mary ADELINE Mountain Horse, as recorded on her headstone (photo on page 83).

Mike Mountain Horse was always my grandfather, and I am proud to say that he still is.

A headstone for Mike Mountain Horse is shown on a current website (November 2021). It is said to be in St Catherine's Cemetery near Standoff. This is wrong. I know because I was at his burial! He was buried in St Paul Cemetery about one kilometre west of the former St Paul residential school.

The burial took place on a cold February day. There was no snow covering the ground, which was not unusual because of the area's warm Chinook wind. His grave lay east to west, and I was at the east end giving me a western view of the Rocky Mountains nearby. The God Guy was to the left. I wondered at the beige coloured soil piled beside the grave and I had a feeling that the frozen dirt had a personality - don't ponder too long — you'll be here soon enough.

No, not soon as I was young (23 years old) and of course immortal[227] and still had many miles to go if I were to experience even a little of life's challenges as Mike Mountain Horse had.

As well as being in the wrong cemetery, the headstone has his age incorrect by about 6 years. And he was demobilized as an Acting Sergeant, not a Private as inscribed on the headstone.

Most unsettling about the headstone is that it does not note Mike's DISTINGUISHED CONDUCT MEDAL (DCM). When I first began researching Mike's history, more than 50 newspaper clippings and articles had the initials DCM after his name. This headstone does not.

---

[227] WOODY ALLEN *"I don't want to achieve immortality …. I want to achieve it [by] not dying"*, The Illustrated Woody Allen ReaderQuotes.

The headstone looks new and out of place in the Saint Catherine's Cemetery. After almost half a century after Mike's burial, I could not find who had improperly placed the headstone. The headstone appears to be a standard army monument, but I can not imagine the usually thorough army making such a mess of it. If they could not get the correct cemetery, what else is wrong with its records, all of which were handwritten over a hundred years ago and now faded and mostly undecipherable.

Given the utter disrespect and bureaucratic impatience with Indians at the time, I can imagine the record keepers during the War writing whatever, if anything, that came to mind. .[228]

---

[228] I have a friend whose last name is Kirk but whose parents last name was Karak until an impatience immigration officer impetuously said the hell with it and wrote something he could spell. Thousands of immigrants to North America had a similar experience. I can see this happening to Indians in the army.

I have another friend whose father's army records were never found.

SUMMARY – "CLEARLY A FASCINATING MAN"

"May the sun and the truth shine everywhere."
(Mike Mountain Horse)

Tom

Page 196 of 256

Mike's youth

The land of Mike's youth is still there, the undulating brown prairie grassland with gentle knolls to the *Porcupine Hills* at the foothills of the *Rocky Mountains*, a wall to everything west except the warm winter Chinook winds that change buffalo-robe freezing weather into buckskin warm days; the winds that loudly bull their way through the tall cotton wood treetops lining the creeks and streams. And, it was empty land during Mike's lifetime, freeing him to wander alone and lazily ponder the stories told by huge clouds that had no regard for the observer, so far below and small.

Roaming that prairie, it must have seemed as vast to a horse rider as the ocean was to a sailor; and his course as uncertain as that of the sailor who depended on the direction of the wind. It is hard to know, let alone imagine, what thoughts Mike had at those times, but certainly they were simple compared to the complexity of modern life, limited to only those things around him that he had experienced in his small world.

But it is not hard to imagine his thoughts when he came back from the War. His mind was now filled with experiences of trains, oceans, people in ships, cities, and trenches. And all manners of shredded body parts lying about.

Understandingly or not, when he returned to his prairie homeland, he committed to treasuring it and those around him; and to not forgetting that commitment for one day for the rest of his life. And that is how he lived to the day he died in 1964.

Mike Mountain Horse was an admirable example of Canadianism without cultural assimilation.

Indian rights

It is disappointing that there is a need to talk about Indian Rights. Rights and responsibilities should be the same for all Canadians — Canadian Rights.

Indian Rights means that Indians have rights that are different than the rights of others. This concept has its basis in what is called fiduciary rights. Fiduciary rights represent the relationship between the Canadian Government and Indigenous people and means that the Government would act in the best interests of the Indians. It was first exercised around confederation when it was determined that Indians needed help in protecting their interests from non-Indians. [229]

The *Charter of Rights and Freedoms* sets Indigenous apart by stating that:

> **25** *The guarantee in this Charter of certain rights and freedoms shall not be construed so as to abrogate or derogate from any aboriginal, treaty or other rights or freedoms that pertain to the aboriginal peoples ...*

Everybody experiences personal discrimination of one kind or another: red hair, gender, clothing, ethnicity, race, too old, too young, too tall, too short, too heavy, too thin, almost anything visible. More pernicious though than personal discrimination is systemic discrimination that is embedded within our society, and there is no more gross example of that than *The Indian Act*. *The Indian Act* is a law of the Canadian Parliament and it perpetuates this discrimination in the *Charter of Rights and Freedoms* (Section 25 – Aboriginal and Treaty Rights).

Regardless of the long out-of-date reasons for Indian rights, they are no longer appropriate for a modern CANADA. In the Charter, there are no rights for Italians or Ukrainians or Chinese or Japanese, or whatever. There are only rights for Canadians, and it's about time Indians had the same rights; or, if that is too hard to grasp then change the Constitution, so everybody has only Indian rights.

---

[229] Originally fiduciary rights where extolled by Indians as being the obligation of the English monarchy to Canada's Indigenous and were paramount to the Government of CANADA. With the patriation of the BNA the obligation fell to the Canadian Government.

To start, abolish *The Indian Act*, which the Parliament of Canada can do because it created the act. This will eliminate Indians, and we will have only Canadians left. Canadian parliamentarians have tried to do this for decades, but Indians have blocked them from doing so. So Indians, if they are are serious about putting a big spike into systematic discrimination, get rid of the legislation that defines the discrimination – it brands Indigenous as different.

It is time Indigenous took responsibility for their own success or failure, and not always crying fiduciary rights as validation for their demands for more money.   It is time Indians took responsibility for their own success or failure, and not always crying fiduciary rights as a source for their demands for more money.

Five billion dollars for recent things like *Truth & Reconciliation* from taxpayers who did nothing to people that it did not happen to.

If anything is going to lead to the extinction of Mike's people, it is going to be inactivity; we are killing them with kindness, providing everything they ask for without any effort from them.

The Indian Act

The Indian Act is a racist law. It is archaic, condescending, and patronizing. It keeps Canadians and Indigenous-Canadians apart. It is a legislated barrier that separates Indigenous from the modern world and obstructs full participation in its benefits, denying each the opportunity to learn from and to share each others' culture. Naming a road or a building after an Indian does not do it.

Giving Indians "First Nations"status is misleading because it implies special status, like first class, and therefore different privileges and rights; and begs the question of who was second, third, etcetera. There is no class structure in CANADA.

It is time for Indians to be Canadians.

The same stigma associated with the name Indian will stick to the new name unless the new name earns a new image. Indigenous have to walk the talk – let their game do the talking.

No beer sold to Indians

He could not buy a beer.

After fighting for CANADA at Vimy Ridge, Cambrai, Amiens, and Hill 70, and being wounded four times, once buried for four days behind enemy lines while a German soldier ate his lunch while sitting on the debris that covered him, Mike came home to Southern *Alberta* where he could not buy a beer.

Because he was an Indian!

But my father, a white man and non-combatant army cook, could. So Mike's Indian friends would wait in their pickup in our back yard while my father went to buy them beer. And wine. Cheap wine by the gallon.

The oil war

The young Indigenous convict stood less than fifteen metres from me in the small courtroom. Between us were the parents of the youths killed by the new truck driven by the Indigenous.

The Indigenous' lawyer was appealing the Indigenous youth's sentence for manslaughter. The lawyer's argument for the appeal was that the youth had just turned eighteen and therefore received for the first time an oil royalty cheque for $40,000. Celebrating, the inebriated Indigenous youth crashed his new truck into a car load of young people returning from church.

The Oil War began the day in 1905 that *Alberta* was created a province by eastern CANADA. The four provinces of eastern CANADA each kept ownership of natural resources within their boundaries when CANADA was formed in 1867. However, the Federal Government kept ownership of *Alberta*'s natural resources when *Alberta* was created.

Thus, CANADA became comprised of two tiers of provinces: a first-class tier (Ontario, Quebec, Nova Scotia, and New Brunswick), and a second-class tier (Manitoba, Saskatchewan, and *Alberta*). This did not go unnoticed in the prairie provinces. Why, they complained and argued over the years, did the eastern provinces own the natural resources within their boundaries and the prairies did not?

To the eastern provinces this was not a matter of any concern they rationalized. After all, the prairies were created by and colonized for, that is exploited,

However, during *Alberta*'s oil war with Ottawa, Premier Lougheed of *Alberta* always spoke about the "ownership of our natural resources", specifically oil, implying that the Federal Government was stealing *Alberta*'s oil. Lougheed knew that this not the case, but in the public media battle between himself and Trudeau, he knew it was easier to communicate, and for *Alberta*ns to understand, simple ownership. In fact, the issue was taxation, who got what share of the revenue from oil sales, not ownership, and Trudeau understood this and was patient because over time, the federal government's legislation was paramount and thus would get the share it wanted, one way or another.

In the end, after a decade of wrangling and bludgeoning *Alberta* with the *National Energy Program*, among other things, Lougheed signed an *Agreement* September 2, 1981, declared victory and went home, declaring that "the pact was a triumph for federalism".[230]

In any case, assessing the share of oil revenues pursuant to the *Agreement* compared to the *National Energy Program,* over the first five years of the *Agreement*, the Federal Government estimated that "Ottawa's share will rise from 24% to 29%, *Alberta*'s share will rise to 34% from 33%, and industry's share will drop from 43% to 33%"[231].

Alberta's change in revenue share is well inside a statistical rounding error — it did not change, which can hardly be called a victory for *Alberta*. The only way it could be called a victory is if a victory is defined as the status quo. The victor is clearly Trudeau and Ottawa at the expense of the oil industry.

Without oil, there would not have been a Peter Lougheed. Money is power, and oil gave him power to play a leading role in the constitution fight. His fight, in the final analysis, was therefore for money.

Pierre Trudeau, on the other hand, did not need oil. He fought for a cause — the future of CANADA. He knew the country needed a tool to fix its unforgiving rigid structure, and that tool was a constitution it could control. His vison and courage gave CANADA a heart and soul by adding *The Charter of Rights and Freedoms* to an otherwise plain administrative constitution, which in the long term will make him Canada's most inspiring leader.

---

[230] I believe Lougheed's use of the word "federalism" as opposed to "confederation" was deliberate because being a premier and a lawyer, he would be well acquainted with the difference between the two words. This is a clear sign, if his action were not already, that his intended path was towards ten little countries, where the provinces held the ultimate power (residual authority) instead of the Federal Government.

[231] junewarren-nickles energy group, oilpatch history, *Trudeau, Lougheed Sign Agreement*, September 2, 1981.

As a footnote to the stick handling in the constitutional war and the role of the oil battle in it, it would be interesting to do a PhD thesis on the distribution of oil revenues over the lifetime of the oil fields.

CANADA archaic country model

Canada' country "model" is archaic. Its structure cries for change as demonstrated by a Quebec referendum in 1995 that kept Canada together by a mere 0.58 percent! This fact is a *cri de coeur*, if not the sign of a crumbling country.

> *To create a new country model, the provincial premiers created the Council of the Federation, for which the plan is to "play a leadership role in the revitalizing the Canadian federation"* [232].

The *Council of the Federation* has been projecting its members' interests by lobbying the American Government, as though the *Council* were representing the intersts of Canada. For example, the *Council* attended the *2018 Summit [May 4-6] of North American Governors and Premiers,* ostensibly "to promote and advance cooperation by the leaders of the federated states of the world's most dynamic continent". In other words, the provinces in terms of authority were being accomodated as though they were American states.

But be careful. Mention the word constitution at a party and you will be amazed how quickly you are standing alone. Use the words job description for politicians and you will be the centre of the party.

---

[232] The Council of the Federation, Canada's Premiers: Founding Agreement, December 2003, https://www.canadaspremiers.ca/about/, June 12, 2020. I'll bet that 99.999% of Albertans do not know what this is, never mind even of hearing about it, although it has been around 18 years and has a staffed secretariat in Ottawa.

The Canada Mike left behind

Mike Mountain Horse's heritage can be seen in the breeze through trackless prairie grass; in unbridled horses pasturing in a meadow; in the forested foothills before the Rocky Mountains; in the scree of a hunting hawk — all reigned over by Chief Mountain, the mountain that looked down on him every morning of his youth ..... and the mountain that he now looks up at every day from his grave.

The Lougheeds and the Trudeaus come and go, but Mike Mountain Horse's timeless spirit will be in the land forever.

He lived the beautiful dream the world has of Canada:

"May the sun and the truth shine everywhere"

Being an Albertan

If making love in a canoe[233] makes you Canadian, then floating your boat in a late summer wheat field makes you an *Alberta*n.

Alberta was wheat fields, long before oil, and will be long after[234]. In the long-term history of civilization, oil, because it cannot be re-planted every Spring like wheat, was destined to be a short fling. However, it was one hell of a ride for Albertans.

Run in circles scream and shout

The origin of the phrase *"When in danger or in doubt, run in circles scream and shout"* is uncertain. Most references cite a military origin, likely around the Second World War. However, one authority quotes a remote Mongolian General as the origin.[235]

---

[233] Attributed to Pierre Berton, famous Canadian author from the Yukon, who denied it but accepted it because it was as good as any other definition of a Canadian, "A Canadian is someone who knows how to make love in a canoe", 1973.

[234] Food and shelter are the two imperative needs of humans, and always will be. Oil just enables people to produce more of them and for more people.

[235] Since there is no consensus on the origin of the phrase "When in danger …", I am sticking with HERMAN WOUK, *The Caine Mutiny*, 1951, all of whose books I have read.

Screaming and shouting has always been a characteristic of soci-ety, in various degrees and loudness. Now, with easily accessible elec-tronic communication, there seems to be much more screaming and shouting than ever. Anyone with access to a cell phone or a computer feels compelled to broadcast an opinion about everything, regardless of what they know, and more often, what they do not know.

Less Government support for Indigenous

At one time Indigenous leaders would ignore the Canadian Gov-ernment by maintaining that their treaties were with the English crown. Well, with the total decolonization of CANADA from England that link can no longer be claimed.

The link with the English Crown passed down to the Canadian Government and was manifested by such things over time as *The Indian Act* and supplemented by what the Indigenous perceived as an inherited Government obligation to them, and the Government's acquiescence of the obligation, known as fiduciary rights.

The Indigenous link with the Canadian Government will become more and more tenuous because of the natural evolution of a more de-centralized country. Nudging this trend from a country with a strong central government to one with stronger regional governments is the *Council of the Federation,* the de facto purpose of which is to replace the federal government. Since its formation in 2003, the council has had a seat at the *North American Governors and Premier's Summit* with the council supposedly representing Canada's interest. (Page 157)

One of the federal interests the Provinces have no interest in is the federal Indigenous file, which some have referred to as chaos.[236] Also, In regard to fiduciary rights, Indigenous People can expect nothing from the Provinces. The bottom line of this is that in the future Indige-nous People will not be able to count on the same of level of support they had from government in the past.

---

[236] TREACY, HEATHER; SINDLINGER, MARY WYATT; AND DAWSON, MAUREEN, *Creating Order out of Chaos*, April 4, 2001.

Why a hero

Mike Mountain Horse was a hero because he successfully lived in two different cultures, one much more dominant than the other. The first culture was his Indian world that was struggling to hang onto the old ways of doing things while ignoring the world had moved on — he recognized this. The second culture was the relentless non-Indian world of mass societies that inexorably rolled on, Indian resistance notwithstanding.

CONCLUSION – "WHAT CANADA NEEDS"

"Mike Mountain Horse was a man ahead of his time ….. [he was] a scholar and historian [when most Indians] were still learning the rudiments" said a preeminent Canadian historian of the Blackfoot.

A current Alberta senior who heard Mike speak more than 80 years ago said "Mike's approach to Indigenous relations is necessary in today's political reality".

His military and public service records speak to this.

"Clearly a fascinating man" wrote the national theatre director.

As his small grandson, I knew nothing of these things, but I still remember his hand on my shoulder in the darkness as we stood by the rail looking down at the water bubbling white from the plowing of the ship's bow, the faint throb of the engines feeling like a heartbeat.

Canada needs more like Mike Mountain Horse!

Canada's Indigenous are sleepwalking backwards into the modern era. They are not facing a world that has changed more in the last half century than it changed in total before.

Epilogue – inexplicable, inexcusable

CANADA has one of the highest, if not the highest, standard of living in the world – by any measurement, especially education and health care.

Yet at the same time, the country has one of the most pitiful and pathetic, shameful social disgraces in the world.

How come?

Disgrace: 54% of children in foster homes are Indigenous

Fifty-four percent of Indigenous children under 14 are in foster care! Incredible e^{237}:.

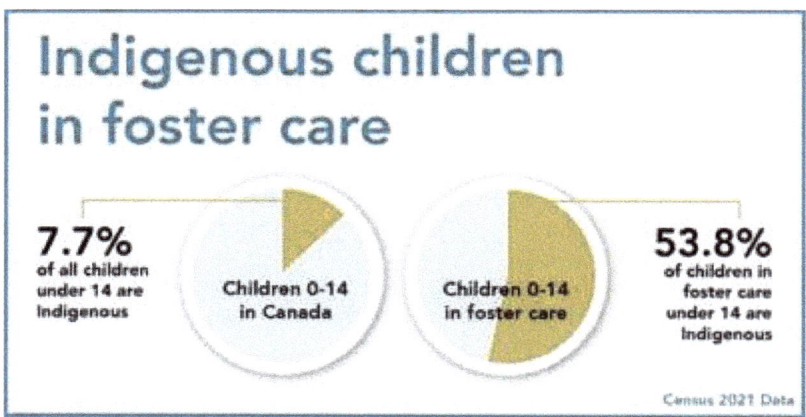

Indigenous children in foster care

7.7% of all children under 14 are Indigenous — Children 0-14 in Canada — Children 0-14 in foster care — **53.8%** of children in foster care under 14 are Indigenous

Census 2021 Data

The Canadian Government expressed shock about this figure.

---

[237] STATISTICS CANADA, sac-isc.gc.ca.

So, what to do? Well, make sure the figure is accurate. Really? The Government establishes an *"Over Representation Index"*. Let's count them. The conclusion: yes, given that Indigenous children are only seven percent of children under fourteen but are fifty-four percent of children in foster care, they *appear* (just appear?) to be overrepresented.

The next thing Government did was to pass *An Act Respecting First Nations, Inuit and Métis children, youth and families*, June 21, 2019. The protocol for this Act is, among other things:

> H *Canada and the Assembly of First Nations seek to reduce the over-representation of First Nations children in care, address gaps in prevention and other child and family services, promote substantive equality for First Nations children and youth, and commit to encouraging and increasing First Nations peoples' direct input, engagement, and control in relation to child and family services;*
>
> I *Exploring fiscal relationships or funding models to support First Nations child and family services in respects of the legislation;*[238]

Now, it is good that First Nations will commit to increasing control in relation to services, but what about committing to more personal responsibility for their children. Surely parents must have some responsibility.

And section H about exploring funding models just sounds too much like throwing money at the problem. There is more than a hundred years of experience to show that does not work.

One thing the *Act* does achieve though is that it acknowledges the problem, but it is not clear about how to solve it. The Quebec Government did not equivocate. It went before the Supreme court of

---

[238] GOVERNMENT OF CANADA, *Protocol regarding An Act Respecting First Nations, Inuit and Métis children, youth and families*, June 25, 2020 (https://sac-isc.gc.ca/eng/1594334398151/1594334464971#:~:text=Protocol%20regarding%20An%20Act%20Respecting%20First%20Nations%2C%20Inuit%20and%20M%C3%A9tis%20children%2C%20youth%20and%20families)

CANADA to argue that the *Act* was ultra vires (beyond the power of the Canadian Government).

The Supreme Court did not buy this. The Assembly of First Nations interpreted the Supreme Court decision as meaning that:

Supreme Court upholds law affirming
Indigenous right to self-government[239]

This ruling was based mainly on section 35 of *The Charter of Rights and Freedoms*, which of course will initiate years of appeals and counterarguments.

However, from a practical point of view, if it does morph into total self government, good, because eventually self government will mean self sufficiency.

Which of course does nothing to solve the problem of overrepresentation of Indigenous children in foster care. One thing that is clear, or though it would seem to be, is that Indigenous parents must at least assume some responsibility for the problem and look after their children.[240]

---

[239] FINE, SEAN AND KRISTY KIRKUP, Globe and Mail, February 12, 2024.

[240] Recently, another cash grab by the Assembly of First Nations (AFN). The AFN claimed that "300,000 people [were] harmed by a system that often-placed kids in foster care instead of offering support to help families stay together". After negotiations, the Canadian Government agreed, with little resistance, to pay AFN $47.8 billion dollars to reform the Indigenous child welfare program. Of this amount $23 billion would go to about 300,000 people who were 'harmed', or about $77,000 each! Head scratching questions: why was it the Government's fault the children were in foster homes? Where were the parents? Why did someone feel something had to be done to help these children by placing them in foster homes? And what kind of harm amounts to $77,000 per child? AFN says they want total control of the welfare systems on Reserves, which his part of their cry for sovereignty. Fine, give it to them; and let them pay for it.

Disgrace: Indigenous in jail

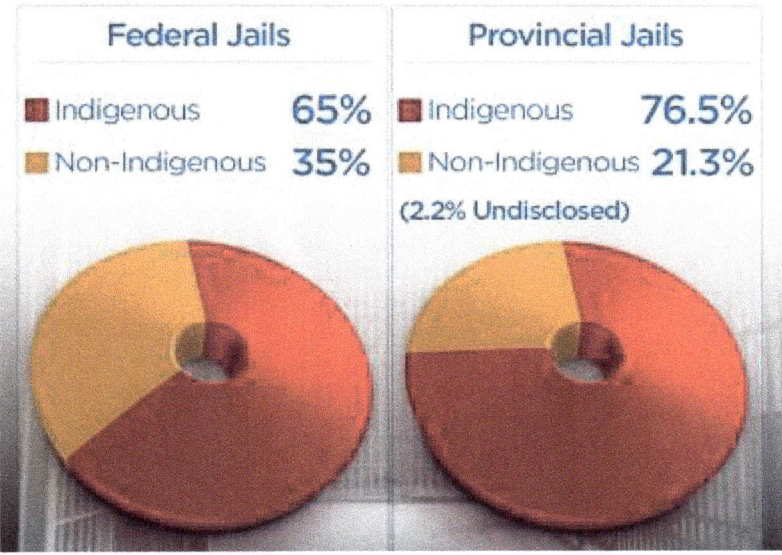

Saskatchewan Incarceration Rates

Federal Jails	Provincial Jails
■ Indigenous **65%**	■ Indigenous **76.5%**
■ Non-Indigenous **35%**	■ Non-Indigenous **21.3%**
	(2.2% Undisclosed)

25 Saskatchewan Indigenous in jail[241]

Oh my god. In Canada, world champion of human rights.

Why are Indigenous people overrepresented in Canadian prisons? Canadian Governments have struggled to answer this question without coming up with any specific cause.

Popular specific answers are like a huge American study seeking to answer the question of why people are poor. After a 5 million dollars the answer was that people are poor because they have no money.

---

[241] GLOBA NEWS, *Indigenous incarceration rates in Saskatchewan*, February 6, 2020.

"People of color [in America] constitutes over 69% of the prison population". (BUREAU OF JUSTICE STATISTICS, *Correctional Populations in the UNITED STATES*, 2021.

Similarly, the Canadian popular answer to why Indigenous are overrepresented in prisons is because they break the law.

While that may be the case, it begs the question of why they break the law.

The Canadian Government's attempts to answer that question has resulted in the accumulation of studies too numerous to keep track of. One study that makes the effort to answer the question is by the GOVERNMENT OF CANADA, *Overrepresentation Of Indigenous People in the Canadian Criminal Justice System*, 2019.[242] This study broadly categories the causes as:

- Colonialization[243]
- Socio-economic Marginalization
- Systemic Discrimination.

Systemic Discrimination and *Socio-economic Marginalization* can be studied indefinitely but they both have their roots in *Colonialization*. Want to deal with them, deal first with *Colonialization*.

Colonialization is embedded in *The Indian Act*. Therefore, to address Indigenous overrepresentation in foster care and prisons, get rid of *The Indian Act*. That's called "tough Love".

To ameliorate the problem, the Executive Director of Public Safety recommends transferring:

> *responsibility to Indigenous groups and communities for the care, custody and supervision of Indigenous offenders.*[244]

This is one of the rare references to Indigenous responsibility.

---

[242] GOVERNMENT OF CANADA, Table of Contents - Research and Statistics Division - *Overrepresentation of Indigenous People in the Canadian Criminal Justice System: Causes and Responses*, 2019.

[243] Blaming incarceration on colonialism is grossly irresponsible. There is no way such an assertion can be empirically or clinically substantiated.

[244] GOVERNMENT OF CANADA, PUBLIC SAFETY, *Indigenous People in Federal Custody Surpasses 30%*, January 21, 2020.

Moving in this direction the *Correctional Service of Canada* has agreed to set up three "healing lodges" to be operated by Indigenous organizations. Not only does this reinforce Indigenous separation from the modern world, but it is also like students marking their own exam papers.

Furthermore, it can be like a precedent. If Indigenous people can be treated differently than others, then why can't Muslims who are calling to have their Sharia Law?

APPENDIX

Figure 26 Mike's War Bonnet

Mike's Story Robe in Military Museums

27 Mike's story robe in the Military Museums

Most records of Canadian experiences in The First World War come in the form of letters, diaries, and correspondence. However, one aboriginal soldier chose to record his war experience in a very traditional aboriginal way, on a calf robe. [245]

The soldier was Mike Mountain Horse, from the Kainai (Blood) First Nations in southwest *Alberta*. Partly motivated to avenge his brother's death from being gassed in the War, in 1916 he enlisted in the 191st Battalion. He later transferred to the machine gun section of the 50th Battalion, *Canadian Expeditionary Force*, for service at the front, and fought at Vimy Ridge, Amiens, Cambrai, and Hill 70. He was wounded three different times but after three years in the trenches was demobilized to CANADA.

Upon returning home, he continued aboriginal traditions by creating the story robe with the help of Ambrose Two Chiefs (the numbers on the Story Robe represent the following panels):

---

[245] The narrative that follows about the Story Robe is from the *Calgary Military Museums*.

No 1 August 21, 1917. In an attack on the German trenches Mike Mountain Horse and his machine gun section came on an old cellar filled with Germans. Mike called on them to surrender, but instead their officer shot and wounded Mike. Mike shot and wounded the officer.

No 2 August 1918. At the battle of Amiens Mike Mountain Horse, with two others, was sent by their commanding officer to scout the country ahead. An honor of this kind was an important factor in the life of a warrior.

No 3 August 11, 1918. At the Battle of Amiens Mike Mountain Horse with a companion shot three Germans who were in a trench. After the other Germans had surrendered, they fired on the Canadians with machine guns.

No 4 August 11, 1918. At the Battle of Amiens. A small party of German soldiers were surprised, and bombed out of their trench, by Mike Mountain Horse' section. The enemy soldiers were shot down, with only one captured.

No 5 August 21, 1917. Mountain Horse was buried in a cellar for four days. He had gone down to get enemy soldiers who had surrendered to the Canadians. While there, a German shell wrecked the roof of the cellar. He was buried beneath the wreckage and left for dead.

No 6 August 10, 1918. At the battle of Amiens Mike Mountain Horse and his section captured a small German hut after killing several of them. The Canadians finished the meal that the Germans had been eating.

No 7 August 10, 1918. At the Battle of Amiens Mike Mountain Horse and his section killed several German machine gunners and captured their guns.

No 8, At the Battle of Amiens Mike Mountain Horse and his section killed a few survivors of a German Battery and marked the German artillery with the marks and designs of the Blackfoot Confederacy.

No 9 August 21. Mike Mountain Horse captured two German soldiers who were patrolling "No-Mans-Land."

No 10 August 9, 1917. While on patrol duty, Mountain Horse fought hand-to-hand with three Germans, killing two of the Germans with his War knife.

No 11 May 12, 1918. Mike Mountain Horse and three companions were sent on a daylight raid on a German machine gun outpost. All the Germans were killed, and one of the Canadians was injured.

No 12 At the Battle of Amiens a huge German shell wiped out all of Mike Mountain Horse's section, but he himself was unharmed.

Mike's pension

"It's a fact, that unlike non-aboriginal soldiers, First Nation sol-diers were not recognized for their service until recently and received no pensions."[246]

First Nations people "did not receive the same pensions or disa-bility and war veterans' allowances as other veterans. …. We also do not have official numbers of honours awarded to First nations soldiers." [247]

No pensions compared to non-Indians is so often repeated that it becomes "fact". This no pension fact is refuted by the document below which identifies Mike's military pension. Furthermore, more than fifty articles and a foreword by a noted Blood historian notes that Mike was awarded the Distinguished Conduct Medal.

However, it is possible that Mike never saw the money because the document is titled Blood Agency. When the Canadian Government gives money to the agency, it is agglomerated in one big check rather than specified by recipient.

BLOOD AGENCY - PENSION OF PRIVATE MIKE MOUNTAIN-HORSE

Archives / Collections and Fonds
File
Textual material

Date: 1932
Source: Government
Reference: RG10, Volume number: 6791, Microfilm reel number: C-8525, File number: 452-525

BLOOD AGENCY - PENSION OF PRIVATE MIKE MOUNTAIN-HORSE. BLOOD-MILITARY MILITARY-BLOOD MOUNTAIN-HORSE MIKE

28 Mike's military pension

---

[246] RICE, MARLENE, elder in residence at VIU's Cowichan campus, Lakr Cowichan Gazette, November 11, 2019.

[247] THE OPEN UNIVERSITY, *Teaching the First World War, undated.* This document does get it right when it states that Mike Mountain Horse was awarded "a Distinguished Conduct Medal".

Cowboys and Indians — Buried four days

Cowboys and Indians were recruited from the *Alberta* foothills because of their assumed superior knowledge of horses and ability to shoot a gun. Those recruited thus became known conversationally as the Cowboy and Indian regiment.

How much Mike when enlisted had to do with horses nobody knows because record keeping for large scale industrial wars was new. Indeed, given the mayhem of the battles and the mass movement of men and matériel, its is remarkable that anyone knew where anyone or anything was.

However, there are some documents, most of which are hand-written and difficult to decipher, probably compiled without regard to penmanship because of circumstances and conditions at the front. Therefore, the Timeline of Mike's service has to be considered with caution. It is a composite of information from:

- Mike's Story Robe in Calgary *Military Museum*;
- The Calgary Military Museums;
- Department of Defence records, such as;
  - Attestation Papers
  - Department of Veterans Affairs
  - Proceedings of Discharge, Casualty Form Active Service
  - Service and Casualty Form
  - Medical History Sheet
  - Medical Case Sheet
  - Medical History of an Invalid, Granville Canadian Special Hospital
  - Form R. 149. 7106-250m-7/2/17;
  - Form DMS 1401
  - Canadian Expeditionary Force Discharge Certificate
  - Separation and Assigned Pay Branch
  - War Diaries, and
  - Among others unrecognizable.

29 Dangerously wounded

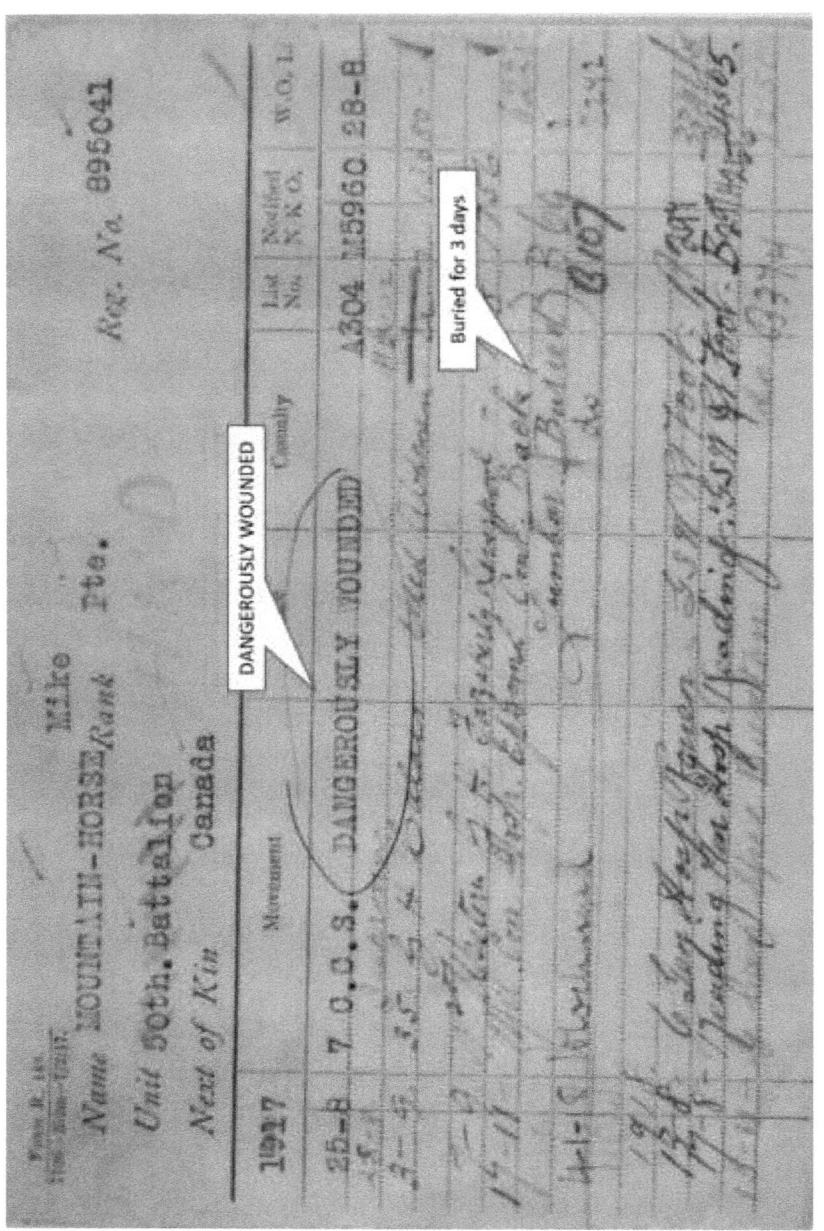

95 Holmwood Avenue NW
Calgary, AB, T2K 2G7
November 16, 1999

> Grady is
> the authors' son.

Dear Grady,

Thank you for your letter of October 15th about Grandpa Healy. My husband wrote his story in the book "The Amazing Death of Calf Shirt". I am enclosing a photocopy of the cover. The book is still available in many bookstores, including the Glenbow Shop.

Regarding some of your specific questions, here are my answers:

The exact place where Grandpa's parents were killed is just east of the town of Sun River, across the bridge and to the north a few hundred yards. We had our picnic there this summer.

Grandpa was not born in Montana. The family had gone down to Sun River to the trading post when they were attacked. Grandpa was a Blood, not a Blackfoot or Gros Ventre.

After the killing, Grandpa was adopted by John J. Healy. This man later was a co-owner of Fort Whoop-Up and then was sheriff in Fort Benton. There is a book about him entitled "Whiskey Peddler: Johnny Healy, North Frontier Trader," by William R. Hunt. It is published by Mountain Press in Missoula, Montana.

Finally, Grandpa was not involved in anything that happened in the Cypress Hills, nor was he connected with the last big battle between the Crees and Blackfoot at Lethbridge.

I hope this helps.

Sincerely,

Pauline Dempsey

> Pauline is the daughter of Mary Mountain Horse's sister; and, the partner of Hugh Dempsey, well-known Alberta Aboriginal historian.
>
> At right is Joe Healy (Potai'na, or Flying Chief) and wife Double Gun Woman, the author's great grandparents.

248

---

[248] The image is of Joe Healy and wife Double Gun Woman, the author's great grandparents.

What do Indigenous want

A definitive and conclusive description of what Indians want is impossible. There are 1,673,785 Indians in Canada, of which 744,855 are registered or Treaty Indians. Less than half (42%, or 329,225) of these registered Indians lived on reserves of which there are over 2,323[249], or an average of about 140 people per reserve[250].

Generally, the most often articulated Indian demand, aside from more money, is that they want self-government, to be in control of their affairs on their territory. Most Canadians would say okay to that, provided self-government included self-sufficiency, like non-Indian municipalities; and, that territory meant the land on which they lived, and not territory said to be "traditional", which Indigenous people in British Columbia claim is 120% of the province.

Finding out what Indians want is difficult, especially because they have the "white mans' political disease" of public consultation: that is, everybody must be consulted, or asked before anything can be done, which results in not much getting done. Consultation ensures that Indians on reserves are stuck back in time while they complain that they do not have the modern attributes of the white society that lives next door.

Their life expectancy in 2011 was about 9 years less than non-aboriginal people[251].

---

[249] Ibid, Melvin.

[250] STATISTICS CANADA, *Aboriginal peoples in Canada*, 2016 Census.

[251] Ibid, Health Reports, Life expectancy of First Nations ...

How many Canadian Indigenous?

Statistics Canada has a broad category called Aboriginal Peoples, which refers to individuals who identify themselves as First Nations, Métis, or Inuit. From the 2016 Census, 1,683,785 individuals identified as Indigenous (how the nomenclature changed from Aboriginal to Indigenous in one paragraph, I do not know), of which 977,230, or 58%, were First Nations. Of these First Nations, 14%, or 136,812 lived in *Alberta*[252].

Indians living on a reserve are 332,675[253] or less than 1% of the Canadian population. However, this does not include "incompletely enumerated Indian Reserves and Indian settlements" where permission was not given for enumeration (for whatever reason).[254]

There are 48 First Nations in *Alberta* with a population of 131,378[255] or 2,737 per First Nation.

In Canada, there are over 600 *First Nations Bands*[256].

In 2017, there were 2,229,820 taxable returns filed in *Alberta*. The total tax payable was $33,313,552,000, or $14,900 per *Alberta* taxpayer. There were an additional 914,820 non-taxable returns.[257]

In 2017, there were 19,400,910 taxable returns filed in CANADA. The total tax payable was $219,388,775,000 or $11,308 per Canadian taxpayer. There were an additional 9,118,500 non-taxable returns.[258]

---

[252] STATISTICS CANADA, *Statistics on Indigenous Peoples*, https://www.statcan.gc.ca/eng/subjects-start/indigenous_peoples.

[253] Other unreferenced information indicates that 867,415 people say they are Indigenous live in urban areas. That is slightly more than half of Indigenous people in Canada live in urban areas. SAWCHUK, JOE, *Social conditions of Indigenous Peoples in Canada,* The Canadian Encyclopedia, October 31, 2011.

[254] STATISTICS CANADA, *Data tables*, 2016 Census.

[255] ALBERTA GOVERNMENT, *Metis Settlements and First Nations in Alberta*, September 2020.

[256] CIRT Business Workbook, *Indigenous Truth & Reconciliation*, Classroom Ready Inc, 2022.

[257] CANADA REVENUE AGENCY, *Income Statistics 2019* (2017 tax year) Final Table 2 for Alberta.

[258] CANADA REVENUE AGENCY, *Income Statistics 2019* (2017 tax year) Final Table 3 for all Canada

United Nations "saves" the Indians

In 2007, 144 countries in the United Nations approved the *United Nations Declaration on the Rights of Indigenous Peoples*. CANADA cast a negative vote, along with AUSTRALIA, NEW ZEALAND and THE UNITED STATES (eleven countries abstained).

CANADA voted no because the *Declaration* conflicted with the *Canadian Charter of Rights and Freedoms*; more specifically, CANADA had "significant concerns over... another article calling on states to obtain prior informed consent with indigenous groups before enacting new laws or administrative measures" [259].

For the *Assembly of First Nations'* point of view, they feel that the *Declaration* is about "the minimum standards that relate to our right to self-rule of our territories" [260].

Indigenous lands and titles

While noting explanations provided by the State[261] party, the Committee is concerned about reports of the potential extinguishment of indigenous land rights and titles. It is concerned that land disputes between indigenous peoples and the State party which have gone on for years impose a heavy financial burden in litigation on the former. The Committee is also concerned about information that indigenous peoples are not always consulted, to ensure that they may exercise their right to free, prior and informed consent to projects and initiatives concerning them[262], including legislation, despite favourable rulings of the Supreme Court (arts. 2 and 27).

The State party should consult indigenous people to (a) seek their free, prior and informed consent whenever legislation and actions

---

[259] CBC, *Canada votes 'no' as UN native rights declaration passes*, Sep 13, 2007. Canada's "no" position was taken by a Conservative Government. A Liberal Government in 2016 agreed to implement the Declaration, although the Declaration was non-binding:

"We are fully adopting this and working to implement it within the laws of CANADA, which is our charter [sic]", (CBC, Canada removing objector status to UN Declaration on the rights of Indigenous Peoples, August 2, 2016).

[260] Ibid.

[261] "State" is the United Nations' way of saying CANADA.

[262] The people of Cougar Ride, a community in southwest Calgary, would have liked to have had this "right" when Calgary Council destroyed a natural area despite a community petition with over 11,000 supporters.

impact on their lands and rights ; and (b) resolve land and resources disputes with indigenous peoples and find ways and means to establish their titles over their lands with respect to their treaty rights.

Indian Act

While noting the position of the State party, the Committee is concerned about the slow application of the 2011 Gender Equity in Indian Registration Act, which amends the Indian Act to remove reported lasting discriminatory effects against indigenous women, in particular regarding the transmission of Indian status, preventing them and their descendants from enjoying all of the benefits related to such status (arts. 2, 3 and 27).

The State party should speed up the application of the 2011 Gender Equity in Indian Registration Act and remove all remaining discriminatory effects of the Indian Act that affect indigenous women and their descendants, so that they enjoy all rights on an equal footing with men.

Indians in jails

The Committee is concerned at the disproportionately high rate of incarceration of indigenous people, including women, in federal and provincial prisons across Canada. The Committee is also concerned that Aboriginal people continue to face obstacles in recourse to justice (arts. 2, 10 and 14).

The State party should ensure the effectiveness of measures taken to prevent the excessive use of incarceration of indigenous peoples and resort, wherever possible, to alternatives to detention. It should enhance its programs enabling indigenous convicted offenders to serve their sentences in their communities. The State party should further strengthen its efforts to promote and facilitate access to justice at all levels by indigenous peoples.

Stagnant situation of Indians

While noting measures taken by the State party, the Committee remains concerned about (a) the risk of disappearance of indigenous languages; (b) some indigenous people lacking access to basic needs; (c) child welfare services which are not sufficiently funded; and (d) the fact that appropriate redress is not yet being provided to all students who attended the Indian Residential Schools (arts. 2 and 27).

The State party should , in consultation with indigenous people , (a) implement and reinforce its existing programmes and policies to supply basic needs to indigenous peoples; (b) reinforce its policies aimed at promoting the preservation of the languages of indigenous peoples ; (c) provide family and childcare services on reserves with sufficient funding ; and (d) fully implement the recommendations of the Truth and Reconciliation Commission with regard to the Indian Residential Schools.

The State party should widely disseminate the Covenant, the two Optional Protocols to the Covenant, the text of its sixth periodic report and the present concluding observations among the judicial, legislative and administrative authorities, civil society and non-governmental organizations operating in the country, and to the general public. The State party should ensure that the report and the present concluding observations are translated into official languages and the minority languages of the State party.

In accordance with rule 71, paragraph 5, of the Committee's rules of procedure, the State party should provide, within one year, relevant information on its implementation of the recommendations made by the Committee in paragraphs 9 (murdered and missing indigenous women and girls[263]), 12 (immigration detention, asylum-seekers and non-refoulement) and 16 (indigenous lands and titles) above.

The Committee requests the State party to submit its next periodic report by 24 July 2020 and to include specific, up-to-date information on the implementation of all its recommendations and on the Covenant as a whole. The Committee requests the State party, in the preparation of the report, to broadly consult civil society and non-governmental organizations operating in the country. In accordance with General Assembly resolution 68/268, the word limit for the report is 21,200 words. [264]

---

[263] In 2016, the Government of Canada dedicated $53.8 million to establish the National Inquiry into Missing and Murdered Indigenous Women and Girls, to complete its important work, and it received additional funding of $38 million to support its extension to complete its Final Report.

[264] United Nations, International Covenant on Civil and Political Rights: Concluding observations on the sixth periodic report of Canada, CCPR/C/CAN/CO/6, August 13, 2015.

An Indian bigot's point of view

This article is an excellent example of why years of trying by non-Indian politicians to eliminate or ameliorate the *Indian Act* have failed. The author of the article states that "the real problem is race-based genocide".

Come on, the world has seen many instances of genocide, and reservation life is not one of them.

The author states that under the authority of the *Indian Act*:

First nations children [were] stolen from their families and nations, while being starved, neglected, physically and sexually abused, tortured, medically experimented on, and left to die. Those were criminal and genocidal acts of race-based violence …

Good luck with negotiating the Act when that is your opening statement.

*"Abolishing the Indian Act
means eliminating First Nations' rights[265]*

by Pam Palmater

(Pam Palmater is a Mi'kmaw citizen and member of Eel River Bar First Nation. She has been a practicing lawyer for 20 years and currently holds the chair in Indigenous governance at Ryerson University.)

"In the 2015 election campaign, Indigenous issues were a central feature in the platforms of most of the candidates. In fact, Justin Trudeau's campaign slogan was "there is no relationship more important to me than the one with Indigenous peoples." He also distanced himself from his father's 1969 White Paper on Indian Policy, which had proposed to abolish the Indian Act, privatize reserves and end treaties. This also helped to set Trudeau apart from former Conservative Prime Minister Stephen Harper whose government agenda was to eliminate the Indian Act and reserves. Yet once Trudeau was elected, his government resumed calls to transition away from the Indian Act, and despite the mass resistance to Trudeau's legislative plans—including immediate

---

[265] Macleans, Opinion, October 2019.

This article is extremely bigoted. If a non-Indian had written it, it would not have been published.

abolishment of the Indian Act—Green Party leader Elizabeth May also included dismantling the Indian Act in her 2019 platform.

May's platform asserts that the Indian Act is "racist and oppressive legislation" that should be dismantled in partnership with First Nations, while ensuring First Nations take the lead. Although she plans to set up processes for First Nations who want to opt out of the Indian Act in the interim, she admits it will be a complex process. In this way, her proposal does not appear to differ much from Trudeau's.

The Indian Act makes an easy target, however, it's not the crux of the problem. The real problem is race-based genocide. None of the platforms make tackling race-based genocide against Indigenous peoples an urgent priority, nor was it mentioned in the last two English debates, with the exception of May stating that she would implement the recommendations of the National Inquiry. The discussion is still about the Indian Act.

The Indian Act authorized the Minister of Indian Affairs (as it then was), to set up boarding schools (residential schools), though there was nothing in the Act that required or even suggested that First Nations children should be stolen from their families and nations, while being starved, neglected, physically and sexually abused, tortured, medically experimented on, and left to die. Those were criminal and genocidal acts of race-based violence committed by individuals and groups. Similarly, while the Indian Act sets out that reserves are held by the Crown for the use and benefit of Indian bands (First Nations), nothing in the Act permits the federal government to racially discriminate against First Nations by purposefully and chronically underfunding critical social programs and services. Those are racist decisions made by people in government, and they lead to lethal results—First Nations have a far lower life span than Canadians.

Yes, the Indian Act is racist; it was designed with the intention of legislating Indians out of existence. In fact, the policies contained within the Act, result in a legislative extinction date for Indians in CANADA . That means that the majority of First Nations who rely on Indian status and determination of membership through the Indian Act also have extinction dates. For well over 140 years, the Indian Act also specifically targeted Indian women and children for removal from their First Nations. The sex discrimination in the Act has been cited as one of the root causes of murdered and missing Indigenous women and girls in CANADA . It is part of CANADA 's infrastructure of laws, policies and practices that serve to devalue the lives of Indigenous peoples. So, to say that the Act is racist is an understatement; those offending sections should, without a doubt, be amended in the interim.

However, the complexities of the Indian Act goes beyond racism. It also serves as a legislative tool by which to hold the federal government accountable for their legal responsibilities. There are various legal protections within the Act, like tax exemptions for property on reserves and the protection of reserve lands from seizure. First Nations have less than 0.2 per cent of all their traditional lands as reserve lands, and preserving the integrity of those collective lands has been identified as a priority by many First Nations. The Indian Act also serves to protect—at least to some extent—from interference by the provinces. This is another major concern of First Nations who know that Indian Act abolishment, without other legal protections in place, means that their lands would be under provincial jurisdiction and vulnerable to the provincial governments' voracious extraction and development appetites.

Yet, despite all of these legal complexities and First Nations historic resistance to outright Indian Act abolishment, governments—both Liberal and Conservative—have continued to push hard on this agenda. Ultimately, the goal of Indian policy has always been the same: First, to acquire Indian lands and resources, and second, to reduce financial obligations acquired through treaties and other agreements with First Nations. The primary methods have been elimination and/or assimilation of Indians (i.e. genocide).

This policy agenda to "get rid of the Indian problem" has dominated successive federal governments despite their words to the contrary. The Indian Act is used as a target to deflect blame for racist decisions made by the federal government while at the same time being used as a clever guise under which to ultimately force the surrender of all First Nation rights. That is why it is so surprising that Elizabeth May would make Indian Act abolishment such a central feature in her platform, when it otherwise makes very significant commitments to First Nations.

Indigenous thought leaders like Russell Diabo have long warned about <u>the dangers in falling for the government's Indian Act abolishment agenda</u>. When abolishment was promoted in the 1969 White Paper, it was for the purpose of eliminating First Nation rights. The same was true when Harper's government pushed for it. There was no promise of substantive constitutional or legislative change to protect First Nations outside of the Indian Act. In Trudeau's multi-million-dollar negotiating tables, what's on offer is an agreement outside of the Act that results in ceding, surrendering and extinguishing First Nations authority and titles in exchange for municipal-type powers.

Diabo is right when he says, "history tells us the real objective is to hollow out and ultimately nullify any rights that Indigenous peoples have to meaningful self-determination." Reliance on section 35 of the Constitution Act, 1982, which states that "the existing Aboriginal and treaty rights of the Aboriginal peoples of CANADA are recognized and affirmed" is also not a realistic alternative, as the Supreme Court of CANADA (SCC) has consistently hollowed Aboriginal and treaty rights through its successive decisions. From Sparrow to Delgamuuwk decisions and beyond, the SCC went from protecting Aboriginal rights as its first priority to making it the lowest priority after settlement, mining, forestry and other extractive agendas.

This makes May's inclusion of Indian Act abolishment plans stand out in her otherwise thoughtful platform which specifically acknowledges Indigenous sovereignty and territory. It is as if she hasn't read the responses of First Nations to the 1969 White Paper by Harold Cardinal for the Indian Association of *Alberta* ("Red Paper"), or the "Wahbung: Our Tomorrows report" by the Manitoba Indian Brotherhood (now Assembly of Manitoba Chiefs), or the Union of B.C. Indian Chiefs response which came to be known as the "Brown Paper." It is also as if she missed the entire Idle No More movement[266] where thousands of First Nations across the country protested over Harper's legislative agenda, which included repealing the Indian Act and whittling away First Nation rights outside of the Act. Had she paid close attention to Trudeau's very public fall from favour with many First Nations, she would have noticed the nation-wide protests against Trudeau's top-down imposition of legislation impacting First Nations and realized that a pan-Aboriginal, one-size fits all approach based on Indian Act abolishment, might not be the answer.

In fairness, May is not the only one peddling outdated solutions for moving forward. Harper's Conservatives and Trudeau's Liberals both made it the central feature of their agendas. While Conservative Leader

---

[266] I'm sorry to reveal that my stereotype of First Nations is so bad, that when the "Idle no more" action was announced, I thought it meant that they were going to focus on getting jobs.

Andrew Scheer has not released his platform, Conservatives passed the Indian Act Amendment and Replacement Act in 2014 requiring the Minister to report on progress made to repeal and replace the Indian Act. Even Maxime Bernier's Peoples Party of Canada platform includes the repeal of the Indian Act to be replaced with laws to make Indigenous peoples like other Canadians and privatize (break up) reserve lands. However, much more was expected of May given her consistently strong commitment to Indigenous issues and the environment. If she hopes to gain Indigenous votes, she needs to throw out the Liberal-Conservative status quo playbook and think outside the Indian Act abolishment box. She might take note of the NDP's platform, which breaks from this Indian Act mantra and instead focuses on working towards Indigenous self-determination without pre-determining what that will look like.

While governments continually say they reject the paternalistic approach to working with First Nations, they continue to unilaterally impose their own laws, policies and solutions. It is long past time that CANADA stopped acting as the saviour of Indians. A respectful path forward that will mean skipping national Aboriginal organizations like the Assembly of First Nations, who are effectively coopted by federal funding and instead, negotiate directly with actual, rights-bearing First Nation governments. Let First Nations decide the way forward and accept that one-size fits all will not work. This might mean some First Nations want to opt-out of some or all aspects of the Indian Act, while others will not. It might also mean that some First Nations are fine to negotiate municipal-style governing arrangements, while others want inter-governmental agreements that respect their sovereignty and jurisdiction in all areas.

If we get this nation-to-nation partnership process part right, then the Indian Act eventually becomes irrelevant, but at a pace which works for First Nations without any risks to their rights. The honour of the Crown and the spirit and intent of the treaties demand no less."

Indigenous beware – the notwithstanding clause

The notwithstanding clause of the *Canadian Charter of Rights and Freedoms* enables provinces to override parts of the *Charter*.

What this means is that politicians of the day can decide what is or is not a basic human right and that a Canadian law can be ignored by provincial legislators.

There is a similar clause in *The Alberta Bill of Rights*. Essentially, This *Bill* states what are fundamental human rights, unless the Legislature (in practical terms, the Premier) says otherwise.

This loophole in human rights is referred to as a notwithstanding clause: that is, a government may override law.

While these loopholes are of concern to many Canadians, they are especially a problem in the long term for Indigenous peoples.

Indigenous peoples have always seen the British monarchy as their ultimate protector ("the great white father"), overlooking the Canadian Government because they feel that Government has not fulfilled promises and treaties. The link or umbilical cord with the monarchy is forever gone with the transfer of the *British North America Act* of 1867 to CANADA.

Trying to prevent the breaking of this link is why Indigenous people camped out in London to lobby the British Government to not transfer the *BNA* to CANADA. The Indigenous people where afraid the transfer would leave them more vulnerable to the whims of Canadian politicians.

Prime Minster Pierre Trudeau tried to allay these fears by including a clause in the *Charter* that essentially says that existing Indigenous treaties would not be affected by the *Charter*. He might as well quietly say into his hat "unless someone says otherwise" (the notwithstanding clause).

Quebec has thumbed its nose at CANADA by invoking the notwithstanding clause in all its legislation. The Alberta Government has put itself in a similar position with *The Alberta Sovereignty Within a United Canada Act* 2022. This act purports to defend the authorities given the province in the Canadian Constitution, which is reasonable, but the word sovereignty takes it beyond just that. It maintains that Alberta's *Bill of Rights, among others,* is paramount to the *Canadian Charter of Rights and Freedoms*.

Provincial Sovereignty is a concept for which the public has not been prepared. The public thinks of itself as Canadians living in Alberta, not Albertans living in CANADA.[267] That is why the Alberta *Sovereignty Act* [268]has the softening addition "Within a United Canada". This is the same political malarky as Quebec's sovereignty act that gives that province's legislature the power to declare sovereignty. However, to soften the starkness of separation, sovereignty is sold as sovereignty "association". The term association is meant to imply that Quebec could be independent of CANADA but still enjoy the benefits of large economies of scale inherent in a larger unit.

There are credible arguments for and against the notwithstanding clause, but none of which are decisive and conclusive.[269] In a way, it depends upon one's point of view. From a politician's point of view, it gives them the ultimate authority as opposed to a court adjudicating the interpretation of legislation. From a citizen's point of view, rights are rights, period, and politicians should not be refereeing them. If a referee

---

[267] People in Quebec feel they are Quebecois living in Canada, not Canadians living in Quebec.

[268] The Alberta Government and The Assembly of First Nations have something in common: sovereignty.

[269] The notwithstanding clause "has been very controversial with very divided opinions. It remains today a current and emotional issue of constitutional significance.

"Those in favour of its removal include [former] Prime Minister Mulroney, former Prime Minister Mr. Trudeau, the Canadian Bar Association, many academics and many commentators ...

"In favour of its retention are some Western Canadian Premiers and governments, many academics and many commentators."

LOUGHEED, PETER, *Notwithstanding Clause?,* Centre for Constitutional Studies, University of Alberta, 1998.

Those arguing either way about the clause often begin by saying "clearly" which usually means its not clear. However, Mr Lougheed, the father of the clause both provincially and federally, is adamant that it be retained. (Ibid)

makes a call the legislators do not like, well, the referee (judge) is only interpreting the law the legislators themselves made.

This implies that the legislators can simply change the law, and in regard to the legal structures supporting the law, they can. But in doing so, much attention must be given to the moral and ethical foundation of those structures. To enact laws that leave rights and freedoms floundering in the wind can seriously undermine the heart and soul of a nation.

Given the new Canadian Constitution and its notwithstanding clause, Indigenous people can no longer depend on historical treaties and promises to protect their rights and property. They must enter the modern world by doing away with archaic laws – *The Indian Act* – and leverage[270] new laws that reflect reality.

---

[270] For example, the Canadian Government wants to do away with The Indian Act. Leverage that in exchange for ownership of Reserves. Reserves are still owned by the Crown. Ownership of Reserve land will entail property protections.

Genocide did not happen in CANADA

Genocide is a term coined after the Second World War to categorize an unprecedented, unfathomable human event — the massive, systematic, industrialized murder of 11,000,000 men, women, and children.

Of these millions, six were Jewish, their murder being called "the final solution" by the murders.

The response by the world was to have a convention – *The Genocide Convention*. In 1948, The United Nations declared genocide a crime but limited it to five categories:

Killing members of a group

Causing group members harm

Imposing measures to prevent births within a group

Forcibly transferring children from one group to another

Physical destruction of a group or part.

This might seem quite clear, but where the law is concerned, a crime requires a determination of *intent* "to destroy, in whole or part, a national ethical, racial, or religious group" (United Nations) in order to be labelled genocide".

The identification of intent, while it may appear obvious, proving it in court has been unworkable. Only a few cases of genocide have been successfully prosecuted (Myanmar, Cambodia, and Former Yugoslavia) while there have been estimates [271] of over 40 genocides causing over 50 million deaths between 1956 and 2016. Canadian Indigenous people do not appear on this list.

The inability to prove intent in court has left a void that has been filled by public and political opinion. The public does not wait for a court to tell it that mass murder has occurred. The dead bodies strewn about are obvious. Clear enough – genocide.

However, when genocide gets into the political sphere, the word genocide is used for shock, not just moral indignation. And in using it

---

[271] The Political Instability Task Force, George Mason University.

for shock, it loses comprehension and undermines the credibility of those using it.

This has happened when the term genocide, in whatever context, is used in reference to Indigenous People in Canada. No type of genocide has happened to them. If it had, they wouldn't be here, never mind they themselves appropriating the non-Indigenous culture around them.

Often the kind type of genocide claimed is cultural genocide. Indigenous have lost, it is said, their cultural heritage because of the non-Indigenous population. In comparison though, Canada is comprised of many cultural groups, immigrants, whose cultures have thrived in the Canadian mosaic.

Mike Mountain Horse thrived. He succeeded in non-Indigenous society while maintaining his heritage.

Morally, outside the courts the public is not limited by any definition and the term genocide is used to lend force to political argument; but the lack of substance to the claim undermines the credibility of the claimant. Given the bewildering array of claims by the Assembly of First Nations, it is convenient for a wearied public to push back by saying no genocide occurred in Canada.

And they are right.

BIBLIOGRAPHY

Books

1. Abella, Irving, and Harold Troper, *None is too many*, Key Porter Books, 1983.
2. Beckett, Ian F.W., 2001, *The Great War*, Edinburgh, Pearson Education Limited.
3. Berton, Pierre, *The National Dream*, Toronto, McClelland and Stewart Limited.
4. Brown, Malcom, *1914: The Men Who Went to War*, London Pan Books.
5. Cohen, Daniel, 1985, *Encyclopedia of Movie Stars*, London, Bison Books.
6. Cook, Tim, 2018, *Vimy, The Battle and The Legend*, Penguin Canada.
7. Cooper, J. Fenimore, *The Last of the Mohicans*, Wordsworth Editions Limited.
8. Crowson, Belinda, *So! You think you know Lethbridge*, Lethbridge Historical Society, 2011.
9. Dr Seuss, 1937, And to Think That I saw It on Mulberry Street, New York, Vanguard Press.
10. Frankopan, Peter, 2015, *The Silk Roads*, First Vintage Books.
11. Findley, Timothy, *The Wars*, Penguin Canada, 1986.
12. Goldenberg, Susan, 1983, *Canadian Pacific, A Portrait of Power*, Toronto, Methuen Publications.
13. Gwyn, Richard, 1980, *The Northern Magus; Pierre Trudeau and Canadians*, Toronto, McClelland and Stewart.
14. Horse, Mike Mountain, 1979, My *People The Bloods*, Calgary, Glenbow-*Alberta* Institute.
15. Hughes, Aaron W., 2022, *10 Days That Shaped Modern Canada*, University of *Alberta* Press
16. Hustak, Allan, 1979, *Peter Lougheed*, Toronto, McClelland and Stewart.

17. Johnston, Alex, 1985, *Lethbridge: A Centennial History*, The City of Lethbridge.
18. Keegan, John, 2000, *The First World War*, New York, Random House.
19. Laskin, Bora, 1966, *Canadian Constitutional Law*, (Third Edition), Toronto: The Carswell Company LTD.
20. Lower, Arthur R.M., *Colony to Nation: A History of Canada*, Toronto, Longmans, Green and Company.
21. MacMillan, Margaret, 2001, *Paris 1919: Six months that changed the world*, New York, Random House.
22. —2013, *The War That Ended Peace*, New York, Penguin Books.
23. Martin, Paul, 2008, *Hell or High Water*, Toronto, McClelland & Stewart LTD.
24. Maurois, Andre, *Disraeli*, Alexandria, Virginia, Time-Life Books.
25. Mulroney, Brian, 2007, *Memoirs*, Toronto: McClelland & Stewart LTD.
26. Radwanski, George, 1978, *Trudeau*, Toronto, The New American Library of Canada Limited.
27. Sindlinger, Thomas L., 1969, *Railway Freight Rate Discrimination in Relation to Western Canada* (Thesis), The University of Calgary.
28. Stevenson, David, 2004, Cataclysm: The First World War as Political Tragedy, New York: Basic Books.
29. Toulouse, Dr Pamela editors et al, *Indigenous Truth and Reconciliation*, Classroom Ready Inc, 2022.
30. Trudeau, Pierre, 1993, *Memoirs*, Toronto, McClelland & Stewart Inc.
31. Tuchman, Barbara, W., 1962, *The Guns of August*, The Random Publishing Group.
32. Vastel, Michel, 1990, The *Outsider: The Life of Pierre Elliot Trudeau*, Toronto: Macmillan of Canada.
33. Warren. Dockter, Editor, 2015, *Winston Churchill At The Telegraph*, London: Aurum Press Ltd.

Articles

(Note: CH is Calgary Herald; LH is Lethbridge Herald)

1. 1910 CH Aug 27, Deerfoot vs Marsh [Foot racing]
2. 1917 Calgary Daily Herald, August 31, [Mike dangerously wounded]
3. 1917 The Gazette, Montreal September 13, Casualty list names five *more local* soldiers [Mike wounded again]
4. 1917 The Macleod News Sept 6, *Heavy Toll of Macleod Heroes*
5. 1918 The Macleod News (Fort Macleod) Feb 21 [While still in hospital Mike wants back in trenches]
6. 1918 CH Oct 26, *Alberta Indian Women Whose Sons Are* Fighting [Mike's mother has three sons in the War]
7. *1918* CH Sept 30 [W. A. sends Parcels to Indian Soldiers]
8. 1921 Calgary Daily Herald Aug 27 [Types of Blood Indians]
9. 1922 CH Feb 15 [Blood Indians Show Interest in Education]
10. 1924 CH Dec 12 The Piegan Indian Lease [Mike argues against legality of leases]
11. 1925 The Herald, Miami, Florida, August 1, Indians Plan Powwow [Mike organizes "The Allied Tribes of Western Canada]
12. 1925 Winnipeg Evening Tribune Jul 9 [3,000 Indians endorse Mike's Allied Tribes of Western Canada]
13. 1925 The Calgary Albertan, Feb 18, Red Men to Show Palefaces How to Stage a Celebration [Indians protest non-Indian compliance of Treaty Seven, the signing of which was attended by Mike's father]
14. 1925 CH Apr 1, Indians to Participate [Mike gets support for Allied Tribes of Western Canada]

15. 1925 Calgary Albertan Feb 18 [Mike organizes North American Powwow]
16. 1925 Saskatoon Daily Star Jun 20, Redskins gather for big Powwow [Mike Master of Ceremonies for 2,000 Indians]
17. 1926 Los Angeles times May2, Discards Tomahawk for Rotary badge [Mike is secretary of The Allied Tribes of Western Canada]
18. 1931 CH Jun 24, Blood Graduates and St. Paul's Old Boys Meet in Jubilee Games [Mike spoke about the early history of St Pauls]
19. 1931 Edmonton Journal, Walsh becomes "Heap Big Chief of Blood Tribe" [Mike serves as interpreter for ceremony]
20. 1934 The Province, Aug 31
21. 1935 Lethbridge Herald Jul 16, Opening of Lethbridge Golden Jubilee Celebrations [Mike Mountain Horse speak(s) over CJOC
22. 1936 CH Dec 26, Redman Writes Western Saga, [Indian history set right by Mike]
23. 1937 LH Mar 12, Lions Hear of Indian Life From Mike Mountain Horse [Mike the public speaker]
24. 1937 CH Apr 3, The Beaver Pipe Legend
25. 1937 The Edmonton Bulletin May 19, Indian Thriller [Mike enthralls children]
26. 1937 CH Jul 22, *Lethbridge Rodeo Proves Success* [Mike the public Indian]
27. 1938 CH Feb 1, His Honour Made "Chief Leader" at St Paul's reunion [250 attend St Paul reunion, notably Mike Mountain Horse]
28. 1939 CH Apr 11
29. 1938 Star-Phoenix Feb 23
30. 1940 CH Nov 16 {Mike addresses school children]
31. 1942 LH Jan 27, Mike Mountain Horse Gives Talk On Indian Lore
32. 1942 Lethbridge Herald, Feb 14, Victory Loan Rally {Indians appreciate their fair treatment]
33. 1944 LH May 10, Stores to Close Victoria Day {Mike is the "star attraction"]
34. 1944 LH Jan 28, This Open Winter [Mike is historical resource]

35. 1951 Lethbridge Herald Oct 24, *Indians Had No Labor Trouble* [Mike, president of local union]
36. 1953 Lethbridge Herald May 13
37. 1953 Lethbridge Herald, June 19, Mike Mountain Horse, [receives railway service award]
38. 1953 North Bay Nugget Aug 17, Mike Mountain Horse: Honoured Indian, [earns fame while advancing in a white man's civilization]
39. 1953 The Sault Star (Sault St. Marie) Aug 13, Indian Made Way in World of White *Man*
40. 40) 1953 Star-Phoenix Aug 19, Chief Mike Mountain Horse Famed Among White Brothers
41. 1953 LH Nov 19, Mike Mountain Horse Retires [A long and colorful career]
42. 1953 The Lethbridge Herald
43. 1953 CH Oct 23, Indian Chief Thanks Army For Birthday [no records existed for Mike's birth, so the army gave him November 11, 1988]
44. 1953 LH Nov 19, Chief Mike Mountain Horse Retires
45. 1953 Calgary Herald, October 24, Children Used Buffalo Ribs for Sleigh Ride
46. 1953 Windsor Star Jun 15, C.P.R. Honors Indian
47. 1955 Lethbridge Herald Feb 4
48. 1955 CH Sept 15, St Paul's Indian School Marks 75th Anniversary, [Mike and Bella Healy (author's aunt) cited as outstanding graduates]
49. 1959 Desert News Mar 21 (Salt Lake City) [Mike Mountain Horse elected minor chief]
50. 1960 CH Feb 19
51. 1967 Press-Telegram (long Beach California) May 19
52. 1979 CH, Jul 14, Books in Review [Mike's book "My People the Bloods"]
53. 1982 Star-Phoenix Dec 24
54. 2003, James Dempsey, *A warrior's robe,* The Free Library by Farlex.
55. 2017 CH April 5 [Mike's military history enshrined in Calgary Military Museums]
56. 2017 CH Jun 3, [movie actor inspired by Mike Mountain Horse]

57. 2014 CH Jun 27, First Nations on the front lines [Mike Mountain Horse became a household name]
58. 2017 CH Jul 14, Looking beyond the past to grasp Indigenous issues [Mike refused to be a victim]

CREDITS

The cover picture is from the *Glenbow Archives*.

The painting of Mike Mountain Horse inside the cover is by Mike Pisko, a Lethbridge artist. It is owned by the author's brother.

The photos of Mike Mountain Horse are from his book MY PEOPLE THE BLOODS or the *Glenbow Archives* in Calgary.

The portrait on Mike Mountain Horse's book is by Gerald Tailfeathers of Kainai.

With thanks, and apologies to those obscured by the fog of the internet

The poem titled *Mike Mountain Horse Message for Modern Canada* (Page 12) is by the Author and was written while in awe of the huge World War II memorial in Kyiv, Ukraine.

The photo of Mike's unmarked grave is by the Author.

The photo of Mike's Story Robe is by the Author.

Twenty-eight books and fifty-seven newspaper articles.

Uncredited illustrations are from the internet fog.

ACKNOWLEDGEMENTS

No one is an island, and this becomes very apparent when thanking those who have participated in producing this book. Where to start, and where, for practical purposes, to end?

I appreciate so many that have helped — a thousand thank you.

And I am grateful that we live in a country at peace and that has one of the highest standards of living in the world.

INDEX

ABOUT THE AUTHOR

In the Crossroads Market in Calgary there is a reward poster for the Sundance Kid. He is described as having black eyes and Grecian features which is, I suppose, related to things Greek. The notable identifying descriptor however, is the line that says he "LOOKS LIKE QUARTER BREED INDIAN".

Well, the drawing of the Sundance Kid is rather nondescript, so to help the reader in visualizing what a quarter-breed Indian looks like, I refer to the picture of this book's author on the following pages.

The author's mother was half-breed and her mother, Mary Mountain Horse (nee Healy, the author's grandmother), was full-breed, daughter of Wolf Moccasin (aka Flying Chief aka Joe Healy) and Double Gun Woman. Mom said he was a scary looking dude but her grandma, who never learned to speak English, was a very kind gentle woman.

This makes the author a quarter-breed, which is obvious from his Grecian features.

Tom Sindlinger spent the first twenty-three years of his life with his sociological grandfather Mike Mountain Horse, which were the last twenty-three years of Mike's life; and his biological grandmother Mary Mountain Horse (nee Healy), daughter of Double Gun Woman: from their unpainted clapboard house in the displaced persons' neighborhood of Lethbridge to the teepees just inside the Calgary Stampede main gate to the Sun Dance at Belly Flats.

He served as a Select Committee Member of the Alberta Heritage Savings Trust Fund, a multibillion-dollar bucket of money representing the economic and political blooming of Alberta. It was a unique vantage point to a short-lived national political transformation.

He was the only Member of the Alberta Legislative Assembly to vocally support the patriation of the *Canadian Constitution and The Canadian Charter of Rights and Freedoms* . His support came after informed conultation and with concern about the consequences for his country if it did not have its destiny in its own hands.

Tom Sindlinger is a Senior Economic Analyst with a focus on marketing and transportation of natural resources, and governance.

He has successfully completed 19 international projects in 12 countries for both private and public entities.

The Alberta and *The Lethbridge Sports Halls of Fame* inducted him in recognition of his Alberta and Canadian basketball championships.

Wow
Food court janitor

Your story is beautifully woven. I love the straightforward simplicity of the [title's] dual meaning.
Performing artist

Fantastic title! It makes you think.
Museum curator

That is one awesome and interesting story.
Former police chief

This is an amazing story, beautifully written, and it brought tears to my eyes.
Teacher

Poignant, heartfelt.
Senior Citizen

This is so very interesting. WOW.
Young Indigenous mother

Mike Mountain Horse's example is a commendable way an Indigenous person dealt with the racism toward him.
Mount Royal University honuors graduate

The title could be changed to "The Unkempt Indigenous Person".
Athlete with Indigenous teammates

The title is not racist because they are Mike's words.
Young missionary in Southeast Asia

The audience LOVED it, as I did!
U of C lecturer

Wonderful presentation.
President national service organization

We need to talk about these things to keep in touch with younger people.
German tourist

Relating and discussing a racial incident is not racism. Openly talking about these kinds of things is the first step to solving them.
Former Israeli combat paratrooper

Lovely ... such an important note in our
history which should be honoured.
International photographer

Wow, I bet there is a story here to tell!
Young soldier

Abrasive and courageous.
Former Treaty 7 Chief

Extremely powerful heart wrenching
story that needs to be told.
Southern Alberta cattleman

I was very drawn into the narrative.
Wonderful work.
Grandson of soldier in
Mike's Canadian Expeditionary Force, 1917

Clearly a fascinating man.
National theatre director

What a great tribute.
I'd love to see the play.
Western Canada university blogger

The poem at the end could be
the lyrics for a ballad.
Southern Alberta philanthropist

The vast majority of people have heard
enough of Indigenous demands
and need a rest.
A prominent Lethbridge leader

You got it right!
A Black Canadian

How can it be said it wasn't
when it can't be said what it was.
Art gallery board member

Fantastic ... [the] message is critically
important at this moment.
Olympic gold medalist

Significant and meaningful.
Calgary developer

People were like wow!
Documentary producer

Incredible.
High school student

This deserves a full documentary.
British film documentary maker.

The poem closing the story
is profound, it is beautiful!
Literary agent

I really really like it. It's a cool story.
Indigenous welder at Fort McMurray